To Rochelle —

中國與美國：
天涯地角，攜手共進

# THE DRAGON AND THE EAGLE

**CHINA AND AMERICA:**
**Growing Together, Worlds Apart**

衛禮
**Denis Waitley**

# The Dragon and The Eagle

China and America: Growing Together, Worlds Apart



Hardcover ISBN: 978-0-9815058-0-0
Softcover ISBN: 978-0-9815058-1-7

BUS069020 BUSINESS & ECONOMICS / International / Economics

**www.hansenhousepublishing.com**

Hansen House Publishing, Inc.
Post Office Box 7665
Newport Beach, CA 92658
USA

Cover design, book layout and typography:
**Chaz DeSimone** www.chazdesimone.com

Cover Dragon and Eagle illustrations:
**Marty Katon** www.katonart.us

Cover Dragon gesture concept:
**Ron Pastucha**

# 龍與鵬

## 中國與美國：天涯地角，攜手共進



Hardcover ISBN: 978-0-9815058-0-0
Softcover ISBN: 978-0-9815058-1-7

BUS069020 BUSINESS & ECONOMICS / International / Economics

**www.hansenhousepublishing.com**

Hansen House Publishing, Inc.
Post Office Box 7665
Newport Beach, CA 92658
USA

封面設計、內文排版與字體
**Chaz DeSimone** www.chazdesimone.com

龍與鵬（封面）繪圖
**Marty Katon** www.katonart.us

龍型（封面）概念設計
**Ron Pastucha**

**謹獻給**

**所有的龍與鵬，以及後世子孫**

二十一世紀諺語：

除非我們記取歷史教訓，
否則注定重蹈覆轍。
還沒有一個社會，
是因為繁榮而存續至今！

我們必須結合東方的智慧與活力，
與西方的創意和實務典範，
以建立全新的交流與合作關係，
並通過時間的考驗。

## DEDICATION

To all Dragons, Eagles and Future Generations

*TWENTY-FIRST CENTURY PROVERB:*

*Unless we learn from history and change accordingly,*
*we are destined to repeat its mistakes, and fail ultimately.*
*No society has ever survived*
*its own success!*

*We must combine the wisdom and energy of the East,*
*with the ingenuity and best practices of the West,*
*and create a new dialogue and partnership*
*that will endure the test of time.*

# 謝詞

**首**先，我要感謝Robert C. Larson，我的一位老友暨同事，本身也是多產作家。他精曉中美兩國的文化，讓本書的兩位主角充滿生命力，也多虧了他的鼎力協助，許多概念才得以付諸於文字。沒有他的才華，本書不可能完成付梓。

我還要謝謝另一個老友葉舒白。他是位優秀的中英文口筆譯工作者。數十年來，我曾多次面對華人聽眾演講，他不但幫助我進一步瞭解中國文化，也幫助華人聽眾進一步瞭解我。他的認真、高標準與謙虛，在在見證了他豐富的文化背景。

我也要向馬克韓森這位跨國企業家、創紀錄的作家及著作行銷大師，表達我的敬佩與感謝之意。他讓我有機會與他合作，把這本小寓言送到最大的讀者群手中。我們都熱切地想協助中國人走出自己的路，同時保有自己的文化信仰與動力。我們也期盼為東西方建立溝通的橋樑，以促進相互學習，創造充滿綜效與喜樂的未來。

我想謝謝韓森書屋的出版團隊，讓我有幸躋身該公司的作家之列。我會盡全力贏得他們的信心。

我還要向位於聖地牙哥的張和榮教授致意。他畫筆下的中國龍栩栩如生，是本書封面設計的靈感來源。

我最後要特別介紹本書的美術編輯Chaz DeSimone。他的設計創意十足，不論是字型和字體的選擇，還是排版與格式上的創新與才華，都會讓讀者覺得本書特別「輕鬆好讀」。

# Acknowledgments

Thanks, first, to my lifelong friend and colleague, Robert C. Larson, a prolific author in his own right. With left-brain English, and right-brain Chinese expertise, he breathed life into the book's two main characters and made a critical contribution in turning concepts into copy and form. This book would not have happened without his talents.

My appreciation, also, to Paul Yeh, a close friend, and one of the finest translators and interpreters of English to spoken Mandarin, and also to simple and formal Chinese characters. Paul has enabled me to better understand the Chinese culture and also helped me to be understood as I have lectured to Chinese-speaking audiences during the past few decades. His dedication, standards of excellence, and humility are testimonies to the richness of his own heritage.

My admiration for and gratitude to global entrepreneur and record-breaking author and mega-book marketer, Mark Victor Hansen, for the opportunity to join forces with him in reaching out to the largest audience possible for this enlightening fable. We both share a passion for helping the Chinese people fulfill their own destinies, according to their own cultural beliefs and motivations. We also hope to build a bridge of understanding between East and West, so that we can learn from each other and create a future of synergy and joy.

Thanks, also, to the entire publishing team at Hansen House for the privilege of becoming one of their authors. I will do all in my power to deserve their confidence.

Appreciation to Professor He Rong Zhang in San Diego for his authentic, artistic representation of the Chinese Dragon, which helped inspire the cover design.

And special recognition to Chaz DeSimone, the graphic architect for the finished product, whose creative design, type and font selection, and innovative flair for layout and format, have made this book especially "reader-friendly."

# 目錄

# Table of Contents

# 前言

# Prologue

從前從前，還是廿一世紀的時候，住著一條龍與一隻鵬。

那是條最為古老、最有智慧且最有力量的龍，體型令人生畏，身長遠達視野所及之處。

根據一個千年傳說，龍前行的時候，尾永遠不會抵達旅程的起點，但循龍行之路者，必能汲取萬千龍足留下的智慧。龍在其遼闊的領土上，備受子民的尊敬與愛戴。

鵬呢，年輕、聰明且敏捷，儘管活動範圍廣大，但只要機會一來，必能靈巧迅速地加以掌握。

據説，鵬的視力是如此清晰精準，所以不費吹灰之力，影響與蹤跡就能遍及四方。從不回頭，鵬只顧著不斷飛向新顛峰與新挑戰，以致不太注意其它國家不同之處。

龍住在遙遠的東方，一個鵬鮮少注意之地，鵬則在西方的某個高峰築了舒適的巢。

有一天，鵬一如往常駕著氣流在天上盤旋時，注意到地平線上有個陰影在移動。這出乎意料的東西不比尋常，令鵬感到不解、不安。

鵬既害怕又好奇，於是收起巨大的雙翼俯衝至雲下，想看個究竟。

一種龐大無比的驚人生物，正從地面的岩縫中緩緩升起。鵬飛得越近，龍看起來就越大。

鵬小心謹慎地停在遠方的樹枝上，以保持距離。起先，龍並未注意到這隻來自天上的鳥。突然，龍轉頭低吼，接著露出算是友善的微笑，示意要鵬做他的座上賓。

於是，龍與鵬開始交談，而之後的對話，就是這本小書的重心。

Once upon a time in the twenty-first century, there lived a Dragon and an Eagle.

The Dragon was most ancient, wise and powerful, with a formidable physique that stretched as far as the eye could see.

A centuries-old legend says that when the Dragon moved forward its tail would never arrive at the starting point of its journey, but that all who followed in the Dragon's path would learn great lessons from those legs that had gone before. The Dragon was respected and loved by all who had populated its vast domain.

The Eagle, on the other hand, was young, smart and swift, with the skill and agility to see and reach targets of opportunity within its expansive territory.

It's said the Eagle had such clear vision and focus, that without scarcely ruffling a feather, it was able to extend its influence and presence throughout the world. Without looking back—and often without paying great attention to the differences in others—it would simply soar on to even greater heights and challenges.

The Dragon lived in a land faraway in the East, in a place scarcely noticed by the Eagle, which now nested comfortably at the summit of a mountain in the West.

Then, one day, as the Eagle made its rounds, circling on the wind currents among the heavens, it saw the shadow of something moving on the horizon. Something unexpected. Different. Puzzling. Disquieting.

Curious, apprehensive, the Eagle folded its mighty wings and dove down through the clouds for a closer look.

Rising slowly from a fissure in the earth was an awe-inspiring living, breathing being whose sheer size defied description. The nearer the Eagle came, the larger the Dragon appeared.

The Eagle, cautious and guarded, perched on the branch of a tree a safe distance away. At first, the Dragon didn't notice this bird from the sky. Then, with a sudden turn of its head and roar, followed by a half-friendly smile, the Dragon beckoned the Eagle to be its honored guest.

And thus began the conversations between the Dragon and the Eagle —and the subsequent dialogue that has become the essence of this first book in the series

嗯，不好意思。我從未見過像您這樣的巨物，所以不敢靠得太近。我在家鄉還算得上勇敢果決，但說您讓我有些膽戰心驚絕不為過。敢問您的健身教練是哪位？

喔，別擔心。我既不噴火，也不是凶神惡煞，跟你們西方對我的描述不一樣。其實，我很樂觀、仁慈且善於聆聽。只不過精力有時還是得發洩一下。您跟我一樣古老的話，就會知道待解決的問題實在太多。要不要下來到寒舍聊聊？

鵰現在進退兩難。他膽敢一賭龍只想誠心聊聊？還是這可怕的東西只想騙頓有羽毛的中飯？嗯，該怎麼辦才好？

鵰最後覺得就算出事，他的動作也一定比龍快。於是，鵰決定冒險，急降至岩縫的入口。

龍兄，您好，幸會幸會。很高興看到您笑容可掬，握爪有力。我還注意到您的巨爪跟我的比起來大多了。哇，您到底多大啊？您為什麼住在山裡？您高壽？我能信任您嗎？您是自己住嗎？您出國到處看看過嗎？您瞭解最新的科技嗎？那…

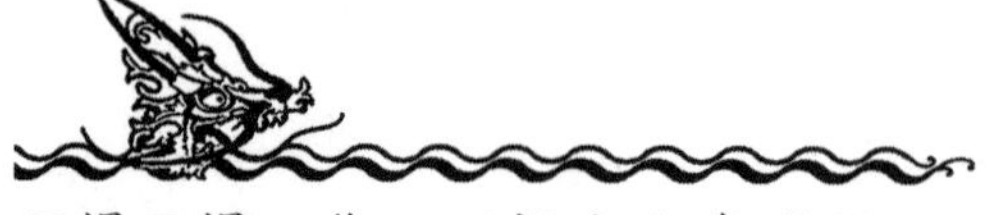

且慢且慢。您一下提出太多問題了，慢慢來。放輕鬆，咱們先喝杯茶。反正還早，時間多的是。我在這山裡住了五千多年，如果真學

Uh, excuse me. I've never encountered anyone like you before and am apprehensive about getting too close. Even though I'm considered brave and assertive where I come from, you really are a bit unnerving to say the least. Who's your personal fitness trainer?

Oh, I wouldn't worry. I'm not the fire-belching, demon-like beast you in the West portray me to be. Actually, I'm optimistic, benevolent and a good listener. Sometimes I just need to blow off some energy. When you're as ancient as I am, there are just so many issues. Why don't you fly down to my abode so we can talk about some of them?

The Eagle was now in a quandary. Did it dare believe the Dragon wanted an honest conversation? Or was this intimidating creature simply hustling a lunch with feathers? Hmmm. What should it do?

Finally, the Eagle figured it could always move faster than the Dragon if things were to get out of hand. So it took the risk and swooped down to the entrance of the cave.

Hello there Dragon, nice to meet you. And thanks for the friendly smile and firm claw-shake. I notice you've got mighty big claws compared to mine. Wow, just how big are you anyway? And why do you live in a mountain? How old are you? Can I trust you? Are you all alone in there? Do you ever get out and see the world? Have you heard about the latest technology? And what about...

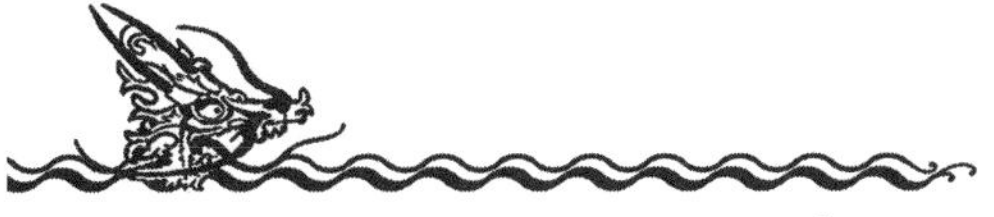

Hold on, wait a minute. You have too many questions. You need to slow down. Take it easy. Have a hot cup of tea with me. We have time. An abundance of time. I've lived in this terrain for more

到了什麼，那就是別急。俗話說得好，*蘿蔔快了不洗泥*。

您的意思，是急的話，可能就顧不到細節，或者細細品味？

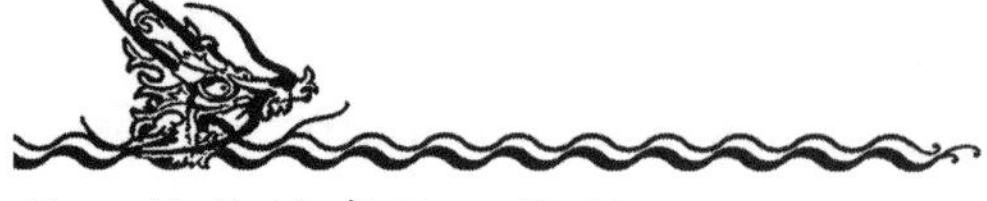

是，就是這意思，很好。

這大概就是我們不同的地方。我喜歡到處飛，看看新鮮事，從不待在同個地方太久。人類「鳥瞰」的觀念，就是從我這兒來的。龍兄，我在這坑坑洞洞的山裡鐵定熬不過一天。更何況超過五千年？根本不可能！

*(嘆氣)*顯然您對我們的歷史與文化瞭解不深。我根本沒隱居過。遠在你們出現之前，我們就已統治地球數個世紀。我集九種龍的典型於一身。九對我們來說似乎是個吉數。九龍分別是：有角的*虯龍*，也是最大的龍；有翼的*應龍*，也是最古老且唯一長翼的龍；護衛眾神邸的*天龍*；為人類福祉興風造雨的*神龍*；保護寶藏的*伏藏龍*；掌管溪河的*地龍*；湖泊中的*蟠龍*；以及現身於洛水，將書契啟示給伏羲氏的*黃龍*。我們還發明了紙、墨、文和書。這些您知道嗎？

than 5,000 years and if I've learned anything it's this: *there's no need to rush.* In fact, in our country we have a proverb that says *Luo bo kuai le bu xi ne.* It means *a dish of carrots hastily cooked may still have soil on the vegetables.*

You mean when you hurry through a situation it may not be possible to attend to the minute details or enjoy the essence?

Yes, that's the meaning exactly. Very good.

I guess that's probably where we're different. I like to fly around, see new things and never stay in one place for too long. I'm the one who gave humans the concept of a "bird's eye view." And Dragon, I'd just die if I had to spend a single day in a cavernous mountain. But over 5,000 years? Unbelievable!

*(sighing)* Obviously, you know little about our history or our culture. I haven't been hiding out at all. For many more centuries than your kind can recall, our kind have ruled the earth. And, I am the embodiment of "Nine Classical Types" of Dragons. Nine seems to be a fortuitous number for us. We've got Quilong, the *Horned Dragons,* our mightiest Dragons; Yinglong, the *Winged Dragons,* our oldest and the only ones with wings; Tianlong, the *Celestial Dragons,* which protect the mansions of the gods; Shenlong, the *Spiritual Dragons,* who produce wind and rain for the benefit of our people; Fucanglong, the *Dragons of Hidden Treasures;* Dilong, the *Underground Dragons,* who preside over rivers and streams; Panlong, the *Coiling Dragons,* who are water Dragons of the lakes; and Huanglong, the *Yellow Dragons,* which emerged from the River Luo to present our legendary Emperor Fu Shi with the elements of writing. We invented paper, ink, writing and books. Were you aware of that?

*（搖頭）*不知道，現在是您說得太多，讓我無法一次吸收了。不過，您怎麼只提了八種龍？

第九種龍，指的是集四龍於一身的*龍王*，這四龍又分別統治了東、西、南、北等四海。

我則是所有九種龍的代表，必須對每位子民的安全、富足和運勢負責。基本上，我住在每位子民的心中。

好，如果您是王，怎麼會住在這洞裡？

我一五一十告訴您，我在這兒思考。這兒不是我的家，只思考和寫作的地方。我對世界的未來感到憂心。我在靜坐沈思的時候，思路比較清楚。茶趁熱喝，來談談您吧。

嗯，我在家鄉被視為山中之王，但資歷跟您的一比就遜色多了。我是家鄉的原住民，別的地方絕對看不到我。跟您比，我實在很小，但跟別的「鳥」比，我可是又大又壯。大家都叫我「白頭鵰」。

*(shaking its head)* No, and now it's you who are offering me too much to digest all at once. Besides, you've only mentioned eight Dragons.

Dragon number nine is referred to as Long Wang, the *Dragon King,* and is actually four Dragons in one persona, each of which rules over one of the four seas, those of the east, south, west, and north.

I represent all nine Dragons, and am charged with vigilance, abundance and good fortune for everyone in our land. For the most part, I reside in the minds and hearts of all who live here.

So, if you are a king, what are you doing in this cave?

To be totally forthright, I am pondering. I don't live here, but come here to think and write. I am concerned about the future of our world. When I engage in quiet meditation and contemplation, I think more clearly. Drink your tea while it's hot and tell me about yourself.

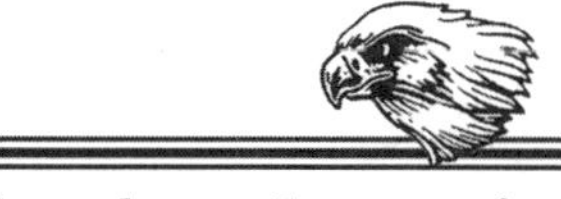

Well, I'm viewed as king of the mountain where I come from, but with credentials that pale compared with yours. I am native to my part of the world and you won't find another like me in any other land. By your standards, I'm small, but by "bird" standards I am considered large and very powerful. I'm known as "the bald Eagle."

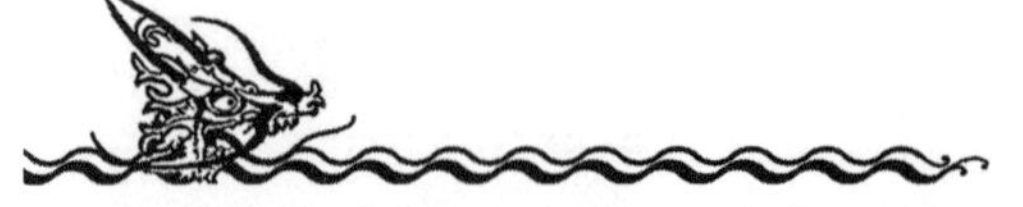

這稱呼還真奇怪。我不知道鳥頭上居然會長白頭髮！

*(著急)*不對不對，跟頭髮沒關係！白頭，是因為我有一頭帥氣平順的白羽毛。獨立戰爭結束後不久，國父們就把我指定為國家的象徵。其中一位國父富蘭克林，居然還公開說他比較希望用火雞當國徽，難以置信吧！

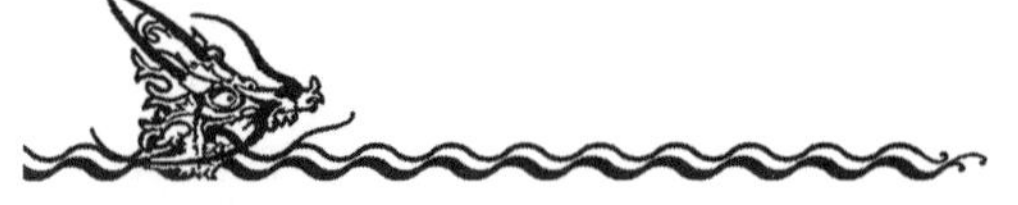

*(咧嘴笑)*若是這樣，我們的對話就會變成「龍與雞」了。還真啟發不了人心。

很高興您也覺得有趣。不過，說真的，支持我的人最後贏了，而我會成為國徽，是因為我代表著獨立自由的開放精神。不但國璽上看得到我，錢幣上也看得到。在此冒昧一問：您的體型這麼不尋常，為什麼會被統治者選上？

這個嘛，有點複雜，但跟我們尊崇「九」這個數字有關。龍有九種典型，每個典型又包含了九個實體，象徵著地球上幾種不同的動物。我的頭看起來像*駱駝*。我的角代表了強壯的*鹿角*。我的眼和*野兔*的很像，但有些學者認為這種說法很無趣。我的耳像壯碩的公

That's a strange label indeed. I didn't know other birds had hair on their heads!

*(flustered)* No, no, it has nothing to do with hair! Bald, in this case, refers to my handsome, smooth-feathered, white head. Our founding fathers designated me as the symbol of our nation, not long after the revolutionary war that made us an independent country. Although one of them, Benjamin Franklin, went on record saying that he preferred our national emblem to be a turkey, if you can believe that!

*(grinning)* Well, then, our conversations would have been titled "The Dragon and The Turkey." Not very inspiring.

I'm glad you found that humorous. But seriously, my backers won the vote, and I became our national emblem because I symbolize boundless spirit of independence and freedom. Not only am I displayed on the Great Seal of our nation, but I also appear on many of our coins. If I may be so bold, why did your rulers select someone with such an unusual shape as you?

Well, it's a little complicated but it goes along with our reverence of the number "9". Just as we have nine types of Dragons, each Dragon consists of nine different entities, representing parts of a number of different types of animals inhabiting the earth. My head resembles that of a *Camel*. My horns represent those of a magnificent *Stag*. My eyes can be likened to those of a *Hare,* although some scholars think that's too nondescript. My ears are

牛。我的長頸像蛇的身體。我的麟像鯉魚。我的腹看似蚌的殼。我的掌象徵尊貴的老虎，且我的爪看起來像鷹，跟鵰兄的很像。

哇，您簡直像個由多種動物一捲而成的綜合體，既龐大又壯觀。我從沒見過像您這樣的巨物。您曾像這樣與其他的鵰聊過嗎？

不曾，我從不多花時間跟他們打交道，但我觀察過他們的行為。很多跟您滿像的，好心且友善，但總在四處奔波。很遺憾的，大部分並沒時間瞭解我們這兒的生活方式。這種行為在來這兒經商的朋友身上很常見。我們畢竟滿不同的：我們是龍，你們是鵰。或許你我可以幫大家做個改變。這不就是創舉了嗎？一條龍與一隻鵰：促進國際相互瞭解的主力！我們只要多喝些茶，聊個幾年就好了。

幾年？我停在同一根樹枝上的時間，也不過才幾分鐘。不過這杯茶真不錯。龍兄，您覺得我們該聊什麼，才能更彼此認識？

好，讓我想想。談談我們的世界觀、生活觀、商業觀、人際觀、家庭觀與教育觀，以及我們的共同未來，怎麼樣？我覺得我們的共同點會比不同點多。

like those of a mighty *Bull*. My long neck is like the body of a *Snake*. My scales look like the *Carp* family of fish. My belly looks similar to shells of a *Clam*. My paws represent those of the regal *Tiger* and my claws look like talons, similar to yours, *Eagle*.

Wow, you're like a menagerie, rolled into one very big and impressive package. I've never seen anything like you before. Have you ever conversed like this with other Eagles?

No, I never spent much time with them, but I have observed their behavior. Many are pretty much like you. Well meaning, friendly, but always rushing about. I'm afraid that many don't take the time to understand how we live in this part of the world. I see this often in the behavior of those who come here to do business. After all, we're quite different: we are Dragons and you are Eagles. But maybe you and I can help change that for others. Wouldn't that be novel? A Dragon and an Eagle: major forces for promoting international understanding! We just need to drink lots of tea and chat for a few years.

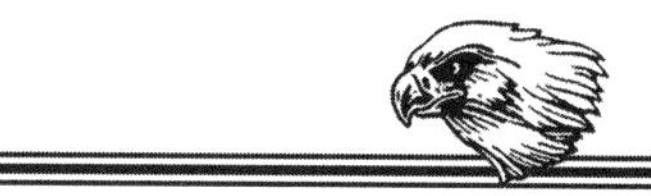

A few years? I've never been perched on a branch for more than a few minutes. But I am enjoying this hot cup of tea. Dragon, what do you think we should discuss to help us better understand one another?

Well, let's see. How about talking about our worldviews, philosophies of life, approaches to business, relationships, family, education and about our future together? I have a feeling we'll have more similarities than differences.

我們說不定甚至有意義相同的諺語。讓我先試個看看。西方有句諺語的意思是「*堅持必成*」。您也有類似的說法嗎？

我們也有，只是描述的方式不同而已。我們會說「*滴水穿石*」。

遠方的太陽逐漸落到地平線下，天空一片燦爛的紅黃彩霞。龍開始緩緩返回地面的巨大岩縫中。鵰也回到棲息的樹枝上，與龍相隔僅咫尺之遙。明天，龍與鵰會繼續他們精彩的對話，或許因此讓我們更瞭解東西方之間的關係。

We probably even have some sayings with the same meaning. Let me try one out for size. In the West we have a proverb that says *perseverance will lead to success*. Do you have anything like that?

That we do. We just refer to this truth it in a different way. We say *di sui chuan shi*...or *dripping water can eat through a stone.*

The sky was now glowing a brilliant red and yellow as the sun in that far-away land began to rest gently on the horizon. The Dragon moved ever so slowly back into the great crevice in the earth. The Eagle returned to its perch just a Dragon's breath away. Tomorrow the Dragon and Eagle would continue their spirited conversation—and perhaps, indeed, begin to shed light on the relationship between East and West.

第一回

CHAPTER 1

# 交個朋友

# Getting to Know You

**東**方的偏遠山區現已破曉。嶄新的一天隱身於密雲及濃霧之後，正悄悄地在這片古老的大地上展開。突然，朝陽如梭般穿過密雲，照耀在逐漸甦醒的巨龍身上。龍伸展著龐大的軀體，好挪到更舒服的位置，然後就像數千年來的每個清晨一樣，慢慢從地面的巨大岩縫中升起。

昨天與鵰談話真有意思。我用了這麼多諺語和故事接待，希望沒把這小兄弟嚇著了。真希望他今天還會再來。

話才說完，龍就聽見震耳的*呼嘯*一聲。古老的龍抬頭仰望，只見新朋友小心緩慢地在上空盤旋，似乎在尋找合適的降落點。

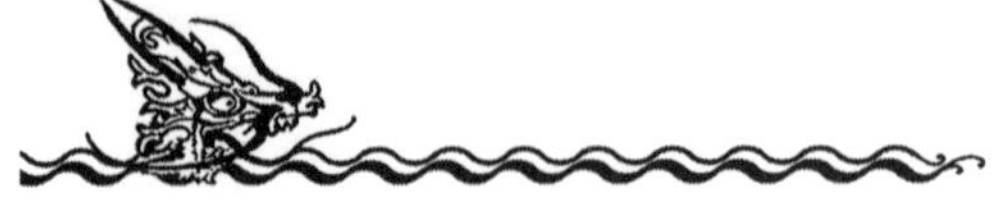

早，鵰兄。請下來繼續聊聊。

於是，鵰最後再繞了一大圈，然後落在離龍首才幾公尺之處，顯然比前一天敢靠的近多了。

早，龍兄。我剛才四處飛翔，不管是上下還是左右，您想得到地方我都去過了。自從昨天見面後，我幾乎都沒闔過眼。您知道嗎，我想出好多全新的觀念想向您請教。有人認為西方是西方，東方是東方，但我覺得這些觀念，不論哪一方都受用。有些甚至還可以賺些錢，但要您感興趣才行。這些新點子包君滿意。不知您意下如何？再怎麼說，我一相情願也沒用。

It was now dawn in a remote mountain range in the East. Shrouded in clouds and a thick, dense fog, another day had quietly begun in the land of antiquity. Then, faster than a weaver's shuttle, the sun pushed through the clouds to reveal the great Dragon rubbing sleep from its eyes. Stretching its mighty body and maneuvering itself into a more comfortable position, it gradually lifted itself from the enormous fissure in the earth, even as it had done for thousands of mornings past.

That was a most interesting conversation with Eagle yesterday. I hope I didn't frighten the youngster by regaling it too much with my stories and proverbs. I do hope it returns today.

No sooner had the Dragon spoken these words when it heard a large *swoooooosh*. It raised its ancient head skyward only to see its new friend flying in slow, deliberate circles overhead as it were looking for a favorable landing area.

Good morning, Eagle. Please fly down and let's continue our dialogue.

With that, the Eagle flew one last, wide circle, landing only a few meters from the head of the Dragon—and certainly closer than it had dared to land the day before.

Good morning, Dragon. I've been flying all over the place—up and down, here and there, you name it. I hardly got a wink of sleep since I saw you yesterday. Guess what? I've come up with a ton of fresh concepts I'd like to run by you. I know they say that East is East and West is West, but when it comes to these ideas, I don't think it matters. Some of them might even make you some money—if you're interested. I think you'll love the new stuff I've come up with. What do you think? But hey, I'm doing all the talking.

嘿，鵬兄，您今天的興致真高啊！可是，有時候，您說的興致好像比聽的高。您要知道，這麼多朝代下來，我們發現年輕的一代若不聽也不尊重長者的智慧與經驗時，這些朝代再怎麼繁榮，都會由內開始崩潰，最後從地球上消失。

我們有句諺語是「*樹倒猢猻散*」。朝代之所以滅亡，都是因為人民並未記取過去的教訓。所以今天只有土裡挖出來的遺跡，才能證明他們曾經存在。

龍兄，我們的文化不像您的那麼悠久，但都出現這些前兆了。一夕竄紅的名人和體育明星，以及為電視精心設計的「偶像」與格鬥戰士，都受萬人崇拜。幼鵰不想聽老鵰的話，只想追風逐電，至於較崇高的使命，像是飛往新高洞察天地萬物，則興趣缺缺。

不過話說回來，這也不能全怪他們。我看他們只是在模仿並反映我們這些老鵰的價值觀吧。龍兄，您或許真說對了。我的確愛說話。我也喜歡在巢裡休息，沈醉在榮登頂峰的榮耀中。我想你覺得自己所向無敵的時候，就不屑聽別人的意見了。

鵰兄呀，不是只有您而已，大家向來都如此。可是，我們得趕緊打破這種惡性循環，否則就來不及了。或許我的歷史觀、堅毅和韌性，再加上您的迅捷和機靈，就能夠去蕪存菁。

我們一定要以此為目標。我們必須保留古老文化的智慧及美麗，並

Ah, Eagle. You are so enthusiastic! However, sometimes you seem to want to speak more than you're prepared to listen. I must say that throughout our many centuries of dynasties, when younger generations failed to listen to and learn to respect the wisdom and experience of their elders, those dynasties—even at their zenith—crumbled from within and vanished from the face of the earth.

We have a proverb that says *shu dao hu sun san*, which means... *Once a tree falls, the monkeys on it will scatter.* And when these dynasties have fallen, it was invariably because individuals failed to learn from the wisdom of the past. As a result, only diggings in the sand remain to document their existence.

We are not as ancient as you, Dragon, and still we see such signs in our own culture. Overnight celebrities, athletes, made-for-television "idols" and gladiators are revered as kings. Young Eaglets, unwilling to listen to older Eagles, focus more on the thrill of flying than on the loftier missions of soaring to new heights for a more intelligent perspective of the planet and its inhabitants.

In their defense, however, I suppose they're only mimicking and reflecting the values of us seasoned Eagles. Maybe you're right about me, Dragon. I do like to talk. I also enjoy resting in my nest, reveling in the glory of being on the top of the world. I guess when you think you're invincible, you don't bother to seek the counsel of others.

Ah, my young Eagle friend, it's not just you. So it has always been. But we must break this terrible cycle before it's too late. Perhaps with my reflections on history, perseverance and resiliency—combined with your agility, swiftness and ingenuity—we can separate the melon from the rind.

This must be our goal: we need to retain the wisdom and beauty of ancient culture and adapt it to a world that is accelerating

把它運用到這個瞬息萬變，連老子或達文西都無法預見的世界。現在一天內發生的變化，就超過於我們祖父母輩整整十年的變化。我們一定有辦法確保過去不再是未來的序幕。

有人說過，所謂荒謬，就是*明明因循守舊，卻指望出陳布新*。

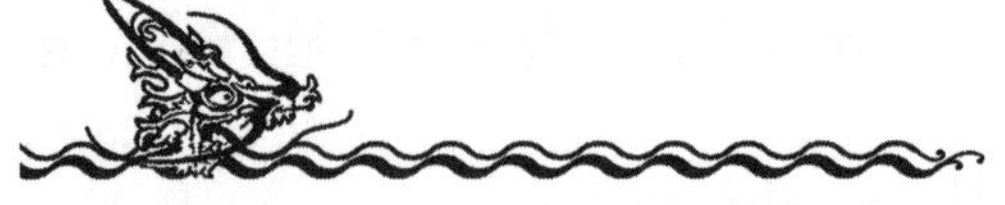

是我說的。而且，我一千多年前就說過了！

龍與鵬整個早上都聊得很高興。他們談過去和未來，談他們對東西方的展望。雙方都決定要全心相互學習，也承認要走的路還很遠。

鵬兄，您在全心學習我們的文化時，必須瞭解我們對自己有什麼看法。首先，我們的領土遼闊。從地理上看，我們位於亞熱帶，與東南亞相連。人口大概有十三億。海岸線將近四千哩，有著許多優良的港口，但我們總是背對著海洋。事實上，我們從未…

可是，龍兄，若非如此，你們說不定已經是個數百年不墜的海上強權。根據我讀的資料，你們一直都具備邁向海洋所需的財富、知識和技能。想像一下，你們說不定已經探索過新大陸，將珍貴的商品攜帶回國。你們說不定已經把經濟與政治力量拓展到其它國家。你

and changing at warp speeds neither Lao Tzu nor Leonardo da Vinci could have foreseen. Certainly there are more changes in a single day than in an entire decade of our grandparents' lives. There must be a way to ensure that the past need not always be prologue for the future.

Someone once said the definition of insanity is *to do the same thing over and over again, and expect a different result.*

That was me. And, I said it more than a thousand years ago!

The Dragon and the Eagle continued their spirited conversation throughout the morning. They discussed the past, the present and how they saw the future unfolding for both East and West. Each agreed to learn what it could from the other. Both also admitted they had a long way to go.

Eagle, as you do your best to learn about my culture, it's important you understand how we view ourselves. First of all, we are a large land mass. Geographically, we are situated in the subtropics and merge into the world of Southeast Asia. We have a population of some 1.3 billion people. With nearly 4,000 miles of coastland, marked by many good harbors, we have always turned our backs to the sea. In fact, we never…

But Dragon, you could have been a major overseas power for hundreds of years. From what I have read, you have always enjoyed the wealth, the knowledge and skill to venture well beyond your own shores. Imagine: you could have explored new lands and brought precious commodities back to your people. You could have imposed your economic and political will on for-

們也可能像今天的西方一般，用你們的勢力和語言影響千千萬萬人。事實上…

…我們沒這麼做，鵰兄。我們反而背對偉大的海洋，以能夠以家立國為榮。的確，我們一向視自己為*世界的中心*。不論對錯，我們自認我們的文化與習俗比較優越，所以經常蔑視那些選擇抗拒的外在力量。

你們仍然抱持這種態度嗎？對你們的文化與文明而言，西方還是一個威脅嗎？

不是，完全不是，但因為這麼多年來我們選擇封閉，所以需要一些時間才能接納外界的指導。可是，若您今天到過我們的主要城市，甚至一些村落，就會發現許多體制與西方的極為類似。這有好有壞。

龍兄，在我今天啟程飛回遠方之前，我想知道東方這些年來改變了多少…同時，不變的又有多少。

eign cultures. You might have emblazoned your influence and language on millions of people as we in the West have done. In fact...

...but we didn't, Eagle. Instead, we turned our backs to the great oceans beyond and we remained content to be a country of families. Yes, we have always considered ourselves to be the *center of the earth*. And, right or wrong, we have often looked with disdain at outside forces that chose to counter the superiority of our culture and customs.

It that changing today? Do you still regard us from the West as threats to your culture and civilization?

No, not at all. But because we chose isolation for so many centuries, it's taking us awhile to accept what the outside world has to teach us. However, when you travel to our major cities—and even to some of our villages—today, many of the institutions you'll see are strikingly similar to what you have in the West. Some of that is good. Some is not so good.

Dragon, before I leave you today for a flight far away, I'd like to know how things have changed in the East over the years...and, on the other hand, how they may still be the same.

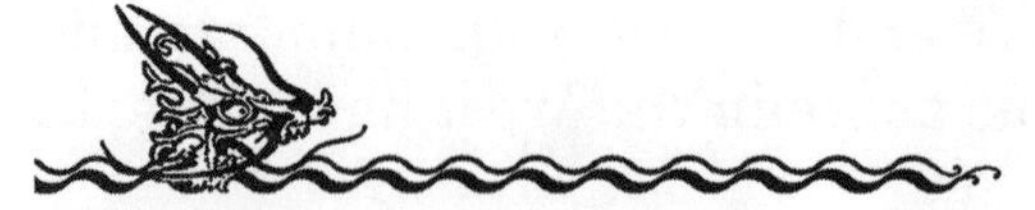

鵬兄，很高興您提這個問題。沒錯，很多事物經歷了重大變革。朝代來來去去。至尊的君王已不再現。哲人與哲學也時興時衰。五千多年，可以發生的事情太多。

可是，有些東西外面變了，裡面卻不變。我們的文化，仍舊崇尚理想化的標準。我們還是能遵循某些傳統的生活方式。

在「過去的東方」，人民瞭解「舉止得體」的重要性。歷經古代哲人的教導，這個觀念已經根深蒂固，況且這些哲人大多是深獲信任的國策顧問。傳統思想告訴我們，理想的社會要從個體追求完美的舉止開始。該怎麼做？則要先從自我追求完美的*思想*開始。

鵬想了好一陣子才開口。這些觀念前所未聞，跟他聽過的相去甚遠。

我開始懂了。東方古代的王朝和君主已成歷史。聖上決定國策時倚賴的哲學家，已消逝在時間的洪流中。但是，從過去遺留至今的影響還有多少？法國人說「*事越變越一樣*」。東方也這麼認為嗎？

在某種程度上是的。東方的日常生活還是看得見過去的影子。禮貌還是要緊。遵守禮節仍然重要。我們依舊重視書面的文字。現代「哲學家」的智慧、指引與意見，也會受到推崇。

I'm glad to hear you ask this, Eagle. Things have changed greatly. That is true. Dynasties have come and gone. Rulers, once powerful and unopposed, are no more. Philosophers and philosophies have found themselves both in and out of favor. In more than 5,000 years, many things can happen.

But some things have not been altered, despite the appearance of surface change. We are still a culture that believes in idealized standards. We remain comfortable living in certain conventional ways.

In the "old East" our people were taught the importance of "proper behavior," something drilled into us by ancient philosophers, many of whom were trusted advisors to our leaders. Traditional thinking for us has always been that an "ideal society" begins with an individual seeking perfection in his or her own actions. How does a person do this? By achieving perfection in one's own *thinking.*

The Eagle thought for several moments before it spoke. This was all new, different, and so unlike anything it had ever heard.

I'm beginning to understand. The ancient dynasties and former leaders of the East are history. The once-trusted philosophers, who ably advised your great emperors, are obscured in the sands of time. But what is the residual effect of your past *today?* In France they say, *plus ça change, plus c'est la meme chose...*which means *the more things change, the more they stay the same.* Is that also true in the East?

To some degree, yes. Daily life in the East continues to bear some resemblance to our past. Courtesy still matters. Observance of correct etiquette remains important. We continue to place the written word in high regard. We also appreciate the wisdom, direction and counsel of today's "philosophers."

這樣看來，您的意思，似乎是你們永遠會保有過去的精華。西方最大的挑戰，大概就是瞭解你們的過去，學習你們的現在，然後有耐性地默默等待，聽聽你們想告訴我們什麼。

龍兄，耐心或許是美德，但西方文化的骨子裡不一定有這個特質。

我待會兒就把這些訊息帶回家，好多幼鵰正急著要瞭解你們呢。可是，龍兄，我走之前，能再送我一句諺語嗎？

好，鵰兄，就這一句。咱們東方會說「*眾人拾柴火焰高*」。我想在西方，就是「*團結力量大*」的意思吧。

鵰點頭贊同，隨即離開龍，飛向傍晚漸漸轉黑的夜色和烏雲。鵰回到遠方高山的巢後，要深思的還很多。

龍回顧了這一天與鵰的相處，也發現大多是自己在分享智慧。龍希望鵰明天還會再來。

龍與鵰。東與西。古與今。歷史、地理和心態，都那麼不同。可是，在其它方面，又這麼相像。法國或許該把他們的諺語改成「*事越變人越一樣*」。

You are saying, it seems, that you'll always be tethered to the best of your past. Perhaps that's our greatest challenge in the West: to understand your past, learn your present ways, and then be quiet and patient long enough to hear what you are trying to tell us. Patience may be a virtue, Dragon, but it's not necessarily an attribute imbedded in the DNA of the Western spirit.

I'll soon be returning to my nest with new information for the many Eaglets that are eager to learn of your ways. But before I go, do you have one more proverb I can take with me, Dragon?

Just this, Eagle. In the East we say, *hong ren shi chai huo yan gao*—which means *only when all contribute their firewood can they build up a strong fire.* I think in the West you would say this means *if we remain united we will stand strong.*

The Eagle nodded in agreement as it flew from the Dragon's presence into the darkening sky and the storm threat of early evening. The Eagle had much to think about as it returned to its nest high in the mountains far away.

The Dragon also contemplated its day with the Eagle. It also realized that it had been dispensing most of the wisdom. The Dragon hoped the Eagle would return again tomorrow.

The Dragon and the Eagle. East and West. Ancient and modern. So far apart in history, geography and mind set. But, in other ways, so much alike. Perhaps the French would consider modifying their proverb to read...*plus ça change, plus c'est la meme personne,* which might then be translated *the more things change, the more the person remains the same.*

# 摘要

第一回

# Summary

CHAPTER 1

## 交個朋友

## Getting to Know You

# 龍親口告訴我們…

# Straight from the Dragon's mouth...

- ☯ 對人生和志業抱持熱忱是好的。然而，此一熱忱，最好能與專注的聆聽相結合。

- ☯ 國家與人民若不尊重長輩的智慧，必會失去重心。

- ☯ 我們必須延續古老文化的智慧與美麗，並將加以調整，以順應*現代日常生活的重大改變*。

- ☯ It is good to be enthusiastic about one's life and enterprise. However, such exuberance is best coupled with an equal passion to listen.

- ☯ Kingdoms and people lose their footing when they fail to respect the wisdom of their elders.

- ☯ It's vital that we retain the wisdom and beauty of ancient culture and *adapt it to the sweeping changes of modern day life.*

## 鵬的看法則是…

# *From the Eagle's point of view...*

✯ 跟東方打交道時，深諳忍耐的藝術至為重要。

✯ 東方諺語反映了數千年的哲學思維，許多仍與今日的東方思維相呼應。

✯ 東方必須瞭解年輕的西方涉世未深。雖然我們的目標大多值得追求，但也應在同時加強自己的敏銳度，以瞭解不同於西方的文化。

✯ When dealing with the East, it is vital to cultivate the fine art of patience.

✯ The proverbs of the East sum up thousands of years of philosophical thinking—much of which remains in sync with Eastern thinking today.

✯ It's important for the East to understand that the West is still young and learning. While, for the most part, we have worthy objectives, we must work more diligently to become more sensitive to cultures different from our own.

# 龍親口告訴我們…
# Straight from the Dragon's mouth...

☯ 我們向來都選擇堅守家園，遵循*以家立國*的原則，而不嘗試成為國際強權。

☯ 禮節有其必要性。禮儀對健全的個人與商業關係至為重要。

☯ Rather than attempt to be an international power, we have always chosen to stay at home and remain a *nation of families.*

☯ Courtesy matters. Etiquette is vital for healthy personal and business relationships.

## 鵬的看法則是…

## From the Eagle's point of view...

✵ 荒謬的定義（不斷做相同的事，卻指望不同的結果）對東方而言不是新觀念。龍指出他幾千年前就提過了。

✵ 與東方持續對話不但可行，而且是必要的。東西方必須相互依存。

✵ The definition of insanity (doing the same thing repeatedly and expecting a different result) is not new to the East. The Dragon told me it said this thousands of years ago.

✵ It is not only possible but fundamental that we remain in on-going dialogue with the East. We need the East as much as it needs the West.

第二回

CHAPTER 2

# 一(不)如往常

# Business (Not) As Usual

接下來的幾個星期，龍與鵰幾乎天天在大岩縫邊見面。不管是又濕又冷、又熱又悶、晴朗還是暴雨…這對朋友都下決心要盡可能時常見面。

儘管鵰比較年輕，生活歷練也不如龍，但鵰已不再害羞。同樣的，龍縱然年事已高，卻覺得跟這位年輕朋友相處得越來越自在。

龍與鵰都搞不懂他們怎麼過了那麼久才認識，才有機會相互學習。他們是這麼不同，但又有這麼多共同點。兩者都認真積極地過生活：做對的時候多，當然也免不了犯錯。

這天早上，彷彿時間一到，鵰就揮舞著巨大的雙翼，俯衝至大岩縫寬闊的邊緣上。

早，鵰兄。飛了這麼遠，氣色還是這麼好。

龍兄，您看起來也不像比我老了一千歲。我常回想我們第一次見面的時候，都不太敢提到東西方之間的重要議題。

您說得對，鵰兄。我們正在建立友誼，而且是慢慢地一天一天來。是耐心和諒解讓我們相互敞開心胸。鵰兄，這還真花了一些時間，對吧？

Over the next few weeks the Dragon and Eagle met almost every day at the edge of the great cavern in the earth. It didn't matter if it was rainy and cold, hot and humid, pleasant or stormy…our two friends made it a point to meet as often as possible.

No longer was the Eagle shy, even though it was younger and had less life experience than the Dragon. By the same token, the Dragon felt increasingly comfortable with its young friend, although the Dragon was ancient in comparison.

Both the Dragon and the Eagle wondered why it had taken so long for them to meet and learn from each other. They were so different. Yet, they held so much in common. Both were living their lives to the fullest: doing things right for the most part, but, of course, each also making its share of mistakes.

This morning, as if on cue, the Eagle flapped its mighty wings and swooped down on to the broad rim of the great crevice in the earth.

Good morning Eagle. You're looking well for flying such a great distance today.

And you don't look a millennium older, my Dragon friend. I often reflect on our first days together, when we were both hesitant to talk about issues of significance between the East and West.

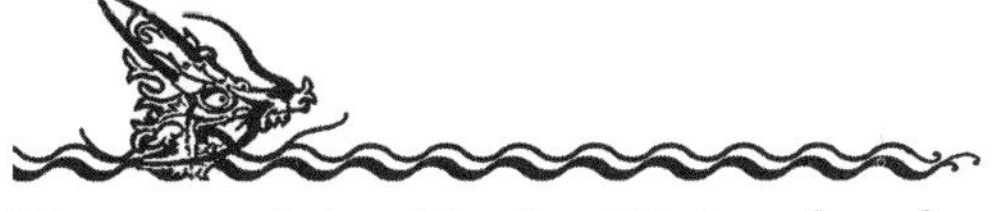

You are right, Eagle. We're developing a relationship, and we're doing it slowly, one day at a time. It's through patience and understanding that we're able to be more open with one another. It's taken a while though, hasn't it, Eagle?

的確，但很值得。老實說，我剛飛越您的廣大領土時，想起兩個問題：*你們在東方是怎麼經商的？我們可以該如何就經商手法進行交流？*

鵬兄，問得好。我的確知道我們的經商方式不同。這不代表誰對誰錯。可是，關注一下不同點是應該的。最適合的途徑，應該就是交談吧。

聽起來不錯，龍兄。您先請，我洗耳恭聽。

首先，請客吃飯對我們來說再重要不過。不瞞您說，吃是我們文化的一大重心。在西方，你們會說：「*嗨，您好嗎？*」我們東方打招呼時常說：「*吃過了嗎？*」吃飯和宴客在商務上也扮演著重要角色。

我們通常是菜一上就敬酒，並請客人先用。我們很用心地招待客人，觀察他們的品格，衡量要不要和他們做生意。畢竟，重要的不光是生意往來，交情也很重要。所以，鵬兄，您到本地經商的時候，絕不能只顧著找合作對象，而是要耐心仔細地交朋友。慢慢來。大家先認識認識。急也沒用。

Yes it has. But it's worth the effort. In fact, as I was flying over your vast expanse today, two more questions came to mind: *How do you do business in the East? And how can we learn from each other's business approaches?*

Eagle, those are good questions. I do know our approaches to doing business are not the same. That doesn't mean either of us is right or wrong. But it would be wise to note our differences. Perhaps it's best if we dialogue back and forth on this issue.

Sounds good to me, Dragon. You go first. I'm all ears and feathers.

First of all, feasts and banquets are of supreme importance to us. In fact, eating is a dominating force in our culture. In the West, you say *"Hello, how are you?"* In the East our greeting is often *"Have you eaten yet?"* Eating and feasting also play a vital role in the business relationship.

We toast our guests the moment the food comes to the table. Visitors are offered food first. We focus intently on our guests, checking out their character, deciding whether or not we want to do business with them. In the end, the relationship with our proposed business partner is vital, not just the business contact. So, Eagle, when you come to do business here, it's important that you not focus so much on finding business associates, but rather that you patiently, carefully search for friends. Take your time. Get to know us. There's no need to rush.

嗯。我們也愛吃。吃也是西方經商重要的一部份。可是，龍兄，照您的說法，有些西方朋友做不成生意，可能是因為他們只想飛過來、找對象、談生意、訂合同然後就回機場。我現在知道這樣為什麼會出問題了。

在西方，關係也重要，但不是決定因素。通常重點放在生意上。事後是不是朋友不重要。我想若只在國內經商，我們的方法就沒什麼對錯…但是…

…但若是兩個文化之*間*有著生意往來，差別可就大了。說了這麼多，我還是認為東方對西方的瞭解，比西方對東方的深。我們是在現代化、全球化，而不只是西化。我們想保住我們悠久文化的精華。

外國朋友到這兒來的時候，通常都太樂觀、太相信人但沒耐性。互敬和平等極為重要。這些原則，是在東方經商的基本前提。污辱和輕蔑絕不能忘，且有仇必報。我們有種求生存的文化，常常誤以為要贏，就有人得輸。這種心態確實在改變，但速度比我預期的還慢。

我們迅速成功的基礎，在於「雙贏」的觀念。雙方都要贏，成功才能長久。我們的理念是「對雙方都不公平的話，不做也罷」。

Hmmmm. We enjoy eating, too. It's an important part of business in the West. But what I hear you say, Dragon, is that some Westerners may fail to succeed in their commercial ventures because they tend to fly in, locate a contact, do the deal, close the deal and head back to the airport. I can see where that could be a problem.

In the West, relationships are important, but not overriding. The deal itself is what usually matters. Friendships may or may not come later. I suppose neither of us is right or wrong with this approach as long as we work in our own regions...but...

...but it makes an enormous difference if our two cultures are going to do business with *each other.* That being said, I still think the East understands you much better than you understand us. We are modernizing and globalizing, not merely Westernizing. We want to retain the best of our ancient culture.

Foreigners who come here often have too much optimism, too much trust and too little patience. Mutual respect and equality are extremely important. These principles are fundamental requisites for doing business in the East. Insults and slights are never forgotten and suffering the consequences is a certainty. We have developed a survival culture. For someone to win, we often operate under the faulty assumption that someone must lose. This is changing, however more slowly than I would like to admit.

Our rapid success has been based on the concept of "win-win." We both must win in order for success to be lasting. Our philosophy is "if it isn't fair to both of us, we shouldn't do it."

*（前後擺尾）*鵬兄啊，饒了我吧！您這麼年輕，難怪會這麼天真！你們的唯利是圖與自私自利，從不輸給任何曾經踩遍（或飛遍）這個世界的國家。

*（憤怒的揮動翅膀）*您怎麼可以這麼說。我們比過去的任何社會都有人道精神。我們提供的援助比任何其它國家都多，但得到的回報，似乎全都是嫉妒和鄙視。我們之所以成功，是因為我們深信只要肯努力，大家成功的機會是一樣的，就連最窮的移民都是如此。您怎麼可以…

等等，不要一下就動氣。我只是想指出你們做許多事，都是出於自身的利益，其實這對世界各地的鵬、龍和人類來說，都是完全正常的

是您的話突然敵意很重，不然我該怎麼想？

*（咧嘴微笑）*我不過是在提醒您我之間的另一個文化差異。我們東方有句古老的諺語「不打不相識」。堅定有主見，是我們尊重的特質，但不要抱著優越感和我們做生意。可別忘了我剛說的，不要取笑我們，或者讓我們既有的方法難堪。教導並示範給我們看怎麼做比較好，才能闖出名堂。

*(whipping its tail back and forth)* Oh, spare me, Eagle! Your youth magnifies your naivety! You are as mercenary and self-involved as any culture that has ever walked (or flown) on the planet!

*(flapping its wings furiously)* I resent that comment. We are more humanitarian than any other society before us. We give more generously to the needy than any other culture, and all we seem to get in return is envy and disdain. We have built our success on embracing the idea of equal opportunities for success for those who earnestly work for it, even the poorest among us who emigrate from other continents. You have no...

Now, now don't get your feathers ruffled so easily. I'm simply pointing out that much of what you do is out of self-interest, which is entirely normal for Eagles, Dragons and humans everywhere.

Well, you sounded so adversarial all of a sudden, what was I to think?

*(smiling broadly)* I was just introducing you to another difference in our two cultures. We in the East have an ancient proverb, *Bu da bu xiang shi...Without a fight, you don't get to know each other.* We respect tough-mindedness and assertiveness. Don't try to do business with us in a condescending manner. But remember what I said earlier, don't insult us or make our system look bad. Tell and show us what would make things better for us and you will go far.

*（慢慢靜下來，收起翅膀）*好，您還真會說教。我只是想告訴您我們能登上顛峰，是因為我們在達成目標的同時，也幫助他方達成目標

我們的新社會確實須要避免過度自私，並專注在雙贏上，不要只顧競爭而忘記合作。別忘了，我們的文化正從「壓抑致富」邁向「鼓勵致富」，從「等公家給」轉型成「靠自己闖」。所以，年輕人很想闖出自己的一片天，出人頭地。

我不是說我們的方式全都公平。我們有所謂的「遊說團體」，這些說客有影響力，有辦法取得官員的許可，好參與利潤豐厚的工程。這些人有權勢，且兩邊都很容易受誘惑而腐敗。

我擔心東方也是這樣，而且規模說不定更大。商人和官員間有默契。政府官員為商機掃除障礙，商人回報的方式，就是讓官員有機會累積個人資產。

反貪法雖然非常嚴厲，但貪污在西方與世界各地似乎一如往常，最近社會大眾緊盯貪官被捕入獄的新聞，貪腐的情形可能因而正在減少。

*(settling back down and folding its wings)* Well, you sure got preachy. All I was trying to say is that our rise to the top has been the result of helping others reach their goals, along with us achieving our own.

It is true that our new society needs to stay away from too much self-interest and focus more on win-win, and from strictly competition to more cooperation. But remember, our culture is moving rapidly from "wealth discouragement" to "wealth encouragement," and from an entitlement society to an entrepreneurial society. And so our young people are hungry to make their individual marks and stand out among the masses.

I'm not suggesting that the way we operate is entirely fair. We have "lobbyists" or individuals with influence who gain clearance from officials to engage in lucrative contracts. These individuals are powerful and there is much temptation on both sides for corruption.

I'm afraid the same is true in the East, only perhaps on a grander scale. We have silent agreements between the business merchants and rulers. Government officials clear the way for business opportunities, and the merchants return the favor by making it possible for officials to build personal assets.

Even with strict laws against corruption, it seems to be part of business as usual in the West and throughout the world. Although there has been so much recent public attention on those who are discovered and punished, that this practice may be diminishing.

我們用*關係*這個詞代表與高層的交情。對我們雙方來說最明智的作法，就是不要讓事業只靠某個人才能獲得官方的青睞。雙方都絕不行賄，因為收買只是一時的。

換句話說，我們該建立的是長期互惠的關係，讓客戶、商人、員工和經營所在地都能獲益。

五千年來，遵守這種綜效原則的朝代，都能夠興盛數百年，不遵守的都很快敗亡。我們應該在交談時反覆強調「除非記取歷史教訓，否則必然重蹈覆轍」。要從這麼多杯茶和思考中多看到些成效，就應該運用影響力散佈這個不變的道理。

我會記得…並轉達我在西方的朋友。龍兄，還有件事。科技正在拉近東西方的距離，簡直難以想像。在西方，今天才買的東西明天就落伍了。軟體的功能越來越強，價格越來越便宜。我們在全力向前划…但還是氣喘如牛…永遠都追不上

We use the word *guanxi* for connections in high places. It would be prudent for both of us to never put our businesses in a position where we are dependent on one individual for access to official blessings. We must never give in to bribery, for no one stays bought for long.

So, instead, we invest in long-range, mutually rewarding relationships where everybody wins: customers, merchants and employees, and the cities in which they operate.

Over the past 5,000 years, the dynasties that adhered to the principles of this kind of synergy flourished for hundreds and hundreds of years, while those who did not quickly decayed and vanished. It is always worth repeating in our conversations, "Unless we learn from the mistakes of the past, we are bound to repeat them." If we gain little more from our many cups of tea and musings, we must pass this universal truth along to all in our spheres of influence.

I'll remember that...and I'll pass it on to my colleagues in the West. Dragon, another thing: technology is bringing our two worlds closer together than any of us could have imagined. In the West, what we buy today is obsolete tomorrow. Software is becoming more powerful and less expensive. We're pedaling as fast we can...and still we're panting for breath...always trying to catch up.

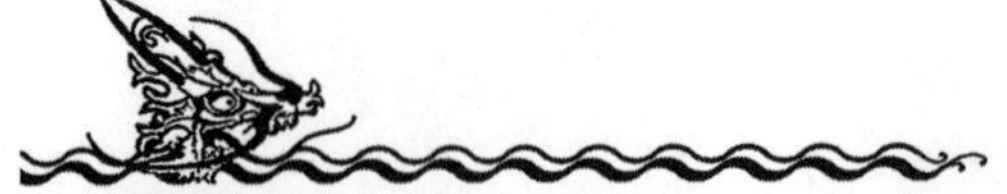

東方這兒的腳步可能更快，老實說，我們的成長前所未見，快得西方商人非得不斷跟上，否則就只能在後面吃灰塵。我綜觀了來到這兒的西方朋友，發現只有極少數具備適當的企業架構，足以讓他們迅速改變思維，獲得成功。

您的意思，是我們必須調整企業模式，重新擬定企業策略？我們不是已經在做了嗎？我們有一些很優秀的人才正與東方做生意，而且大多很有實力，這一點我非常確定。

鵰兄，西方商人的聰明才智，並不是問題所在。我只是認為你們對我們要再敏銳些，我們對你們也是一樣。沒錯，不論是哪個方面，我們的進展都快得不像話。我們的製造與生產力，目前遠優於我們的管理與訓練系統，所以進程才缺乏效率。

可是，你們的進展還是驚人，龍兄。每次飛過你們的城市或村落，我都看到進步。

鵰兄，謝謝您的肯定。儘管如此，企業由公營轉民營的同時，我們對有巧思的創投工具不夠瞭解，也不會運用。許多國內經理人的能力，還不足以讓他們有自信地走上國際舞台。我們封閉了太久，以

And events here in the East may be moving even faster—so swiftly, in fact, that unless Western business people make the continued effort to stay abreast of our unprecedented growth, they may be left in the dust. As I survey the landscape of Westerners coming here, I sense that too few have the corporate framework to re-tool their thinking as quickly as they must to be successful.

Do you mean we need to modify our business models and re-work our business strategies? Aren't we already doing this? We have bright, intelligent people doing business with the East who, for the most part, know what they're doing. I know this for a fact.

Eagle, the intelligence of business people in the West is not in question. I'm simply saying that you must be as sensitive to us as we must be sensitive to you. Yes, we are moving at breakneck speed on every front. Our manufacturing and production ability is far ahead of our management and training systems to make the processes flow efficiently.

But you are making incredible progress, Dragon. I can see it every time I fly over one of your cities or villages.

Thank you, Eagle, for your affirmation. Still, in the transition from government-sponsored businesses to privately-owned businesses, we are behind in our understanding and employment of creative venture capitalism. And many of our regional managers are not well equipped to work confidently on the international scene.

致今天真正的挑戰，在於如何更有效地交換不同看法。這就是我們能從外來經驗獲益的地方。

是的，這也是我們為什麼要繼續常聚聚的原因之一。這種交流對雙方都好處多多。管理方法、信心建立、客戶服務和創意行銷等方面，我們應該幫得上忙。可是，一向由上而下的團隊合作模式，要轉變成自動自發的模式，對你們來說一定不容易。

鵬兄，這不成問題。在大海的這一邊，事情從沒簡單過。這麼多世紀以來，我們奮力苦撐往上爬，最後都一定成功。可是在這個新經濟時代，甚至我們這個古老的龍族，都得承認沒朋友幫忙是不行通的。

龍兄，這想當然爾，但老實說，我們真的不太敢跟你們分享我們的技術。西方最擔心的，就是所有的製造業都幾乎已經移到東方。因為龍的數量以億計算，所以你們可以用我們根本比不上的低成本，把完工的產品再出口給我們。我們正在變成一群以服務業為主的消費者，而不是生產者。鵬族因此感到非常不安，並考慮用新的關稅與貿易障礙等反擊，心態已幾近保護主義與自我防衛。我們擔心生活水準會下降，而你們的將上揚。

We have lived inward for so long that our real challenge is to network more effectively with other points of view. This is where we can benefit from outside experience.

Yes, that's one of the reasons we must keep getting together. We have much to gain from this kind of interaction. We possibly can help you with management methods, confidence building, customer service attitudes and innovative marketing. Moving from a top-down hierarchy to self-directed teamwork won't be easy for you, however.

Eagle, this does not bother us. Nothing has ever been easy on this side of the great oceans. We've struggled and strained to be the best we can be for centuries, and, in the end, we've always been successful. But in this new economic atmosphere, even this old Dragon society is admitting it needs assistance.

I'm sure this is true, Dragon, but I must admit that we have some reservations in sharing our know-how with you in these areas. Something that is of the greatest concern to the West is the flight of virtually all manufacturing jobs to the East. Because you have so many millions of Dragons, you can produce and export products back to us and the rest of the world at costs that make us totally non-competitive. We are becoming a service-industry society of consumers, instead of producers. This is causing great unrest among the Eagle population and a backlash that borders on protectionism and self-defense with new tariffs and trade barriers being considered. We are afraid our standard of living will suffer, while yours will flourish.

*（聳肩嘆氣）*這真是千古不變。「貧者」飢餓羨慕地看著「富者」桌上的大餐。我們不眠不休地拼命製造和出口，最後能帶給家人的，只不過是你們收入的零頭。所以不論是讀書、學習、工作和生產，我們都要比競爭對手還強，因為我們迫不及待地想分到足夠的全球大餅，好養育這一代及後代。

龍兄，您說得一針見血。這就是為什麼您和另外十幾億的龍，對西方來說既是威脅又是啟示。我自己則當然希望我們的友誼有所啟示。您覺得這可能嗎？

年輕的龍知道，從今天開始，知識會是這個世紀與未來的主宰。不論是夜晚、週末還是放假，他們都把握時間唸書。他們很用功地學習你們的語言，因為它是目前經商及各類專業的主要用語。我勸您也提醒幼鵰：學習我們的語言，是個明智的決定

我們有些大學是全世界最好的，讓學生有機會研習各種科目，從科學、文學、商學、表演到藝術應有盡有。這一直是我們成功的象徵。你們有成千上萬的幼龍，正在和我們的幼鵰一起學習。

*(with a shrug and a sigh)* And so it has always been throughout history. The "have-nots" are hungry and look with envy on the banquet tables of the "haves." We toil for pennies, 24/7, to produce and export goods that will reward our families with but a fraction of your take-home pay. So we must out-study, out-learn, out-work, and out-produce the competition because of the inexorable yearning for enough of a share of the world pie to nourish this and future generations.

You've hit the nail on the head, Dragon. That's why you and your one billion-plus Dragons are both a threat and an inspiration to the West. Personally, I'd rather we have an "inspired" relationship. Do you think that's possible?

Our young Dragons realize that knowledge will rule the remainder of this century and those to follow. They devote much of their free time to studying at night, on weekends and during their short vacations. They expend great effort into learning your language, which, for the present, is the language of business and the professions. I urge you to suggest to your young Eagles that it would be prudent for them to learn our language as well.

But we have some of the finest universities in the world, which offer our students the opportunity to become versed in everything from the sciences, literature, and business to the performing and fine arts. This has always been a hallmark of our success. And your young Dragons come by the thousands to learn alongside our Eaglets.

西方的大學體系，無疑是學習的絕佳管道。這兒考不上大學的學生，必須到其它國家尋求高等教育。辛苦幫孩子存學費到貴國留學的家庭，都很樂意把孩子送出國，好強化他們的人力資本。

以前，從你們大學畢業的幼龍，會為了較好的工作機會留在西方。您應該也看得出來這個趨勢正在轉變中。幼龍現在願意回到東方，因為這兒的工作很多，領高薪的機會也高多了。

我們每年有一百多萬大學畢業生，其中大概七萬主修的是科技，也就是我們最擅長的領域。你們的狀況呢？

你們在科技上的創造力和獨創性令人嘖嘖稱奇。你們銷售的產品和服務，讓我們佩服不已。

為了跟上，我們每年有超過四百萬大學畢業生，其中約有一百萬主修科技。我們知道要縮短科技領域上的差距，唯有培養大量已經準備就緒的年輕朋友，向你們學習怎麼「跳脫既有思維」。

好幾百年前，我們之所以故步自封，是因為我們只想保護自己的技術和文化，而不願到國境之外散播。不管是誰，都沒法兒擋住人力資本的浪潮，而人力資本的價值，在於知識與技能，以及為大眾提供價廉物美的產品與服務。

There is no question that you in the West have a marvelous vehicle for learning in your university system. Those students who do not qualify for entrance into our system must look to other countries for their advanced education. Families who have sacrificed to save enough to help their children afford your tuition fees, gladly send their children abroad to strengthen their human capital.

In the past, many young Dragons who graduated from your universities remained in the West because of the favorable job opportunities. You will see that trend reversing as the young Dragons return home to the East, where the jobs are becoming plentiful and the income potential much higher.

We have over one million university graduates each year, with about seventy thousand of them in the science and technology fields, where we have excelled. What about you?

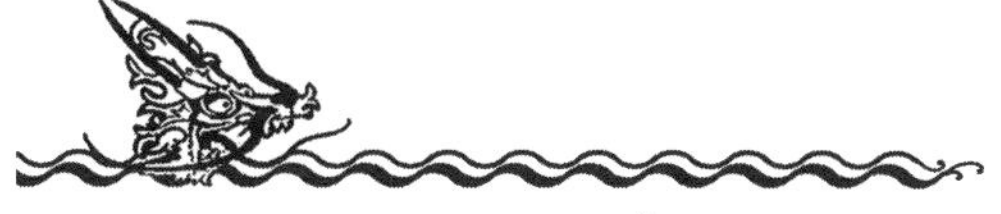

Your inventiveness and ingenuity in the fields of science and technology are legendary. You create and sell products and services that the rest of us hold in awe.

For us to compete, we are graduating over four million Dragons from our universities each year, with nearly one million of them in the science and technology fields. We know that closing the gap in these fields depends upon sheer numbers of our young people being prepared and then learning from you how to, as you would say, "think outside the box."

What stifled us centuries earlier was protecting rather than projecting our skills and culture beyond our borders. There is nothing you or anyone else can do to stem the tide of human capital whose value is in knowledge, skills and production of superior products and services at affordable prices for the masses.

所以，在商業與貿易上，我們終究居住在一個無國境的世界。因為我們能快速地取得訊息，所以知識不會集中在某個地區或社會。知識與應用是全新的主宰力量。除非我們能跑在變化的前鋒，否則就會被速度快者踐踏。龍兄，昨天的世界紀錄，今天只是最低門檻而已。您說是不是？

老兄，說得好。您絕對不要在西方的高峰上休息太久，只顧心滿意足地看著自己的領土。不管是從我們以及從過去的帝國，還是從體育王朝、事業王朝或家庭王朝身上，您都一定已經學到自滿只會滋長放任、懶惰和不勞而獲的心態。您不會因為您是鵰，就能自動永保第一，您必須重新當一隻飢渴、靈敏、好奇且好學的鵰。

龍兄，我飛回西方之前要提醒您：一旦龍族嚐到物質上的成就，體會到幸福的滋味後，就應該從我們身上學到：邁向富足之路似乎還很長遠，但優越感和愛享樂的現象很快就會出現。孩子的企圖心，其實反映了我們的價值。

我們已全部變成一群消費者，而不是努力不斷追求進步的生產者。你們的孩子，很快就會在各個層面出類拔萃，但卻忘了父母栽培他們時付出的心力。

這個道理不用學歷史都能明白。只要上網或觀察我們的娛樂方式，就不難看出今天外表比實力重要。我們一下就忘了當初是怎麼成為第一的

So the bottom line is that we live in a borderless world as far as business and commerce are concerned. And because of instant access to information, there is no concentration of knowledge in any geographic location or society. Knowledge and its employment are the new dominant forces. Unless we are on the leading edge of change, we will be trampled by those who are running faster. I guess we can say with certainty, Dragon, that "Yesterday's world records are today's entry level requirements?"

Well said, my friend. And you must never rest too long on your mountain peak in the West, surveying your domain and remaining satisfied. Certainly you have learned from us, from other empires past, from sports, business and family dynasties, that complacency breeds indulgence and laziness, and an entitlement mentality. You will not remain on top, simply because you are an Eagle. You will remain on top if you become, once again, a hungry, agile, curious, and apprentice Eagle.

And, before I fly away to the West again, my dear Dragon, I must also caution you that once your Dragons taste success in the form of material goods to give them a sense of well-being, you should learn from us that although the journey to riches seems long in arriving, the feeling of superiority and enjoying the bounties sets in very rapidly. Our children's ambitions are a reflection of our adult values.

We have become a society of consumers, instead of dedicating ourselves to continuous improvement as producers. It won't take long for your children to enjoy the taste of excellence in all things, while forgetting the effort and dedication that their parents put forth to make them possible.

You don't have to study ancient history to learn this. You only need to go online or witness how we entertain ourselves to see that style is winning over substance. We are fast to forget what got us to the top in the first place.

鵬兄，我們一定要記住這些話，並在往後見面時反覆強調。變化的速度，讓你我都沒辦法坐視不管。你們必須重拾拓荒的慾望，而我們雖須滿足慾望，但要不貪不懶。

你們要從一群消費者，轉變成一群生產者，而我們要從一群生產者，轉變成一群創新的技術開發者。

你我都要*相互*保持耐心，但對自己和自身的成就不能有耐性。我們要隨時準備好，一旦有必要，就能調整方法和流程，同時記得「*遠水救不了近火*」這句古老的諺語。

*（開始起飛，喊出心中的想法）*「貧者」必須有機會充分學習，來得到「富者」所享有的。有件事很確定：知識和行動主宰著你我的未來。

鵬已消失在雲中，龍則慢慢地滑回地面上的大岩縫中，回想遙遠的過去，並思考如何迎接更美好的未來。任何一隻認為龍在冬眠的鵬，風險可得自負了。龍清醒得很，且根本不覺得累。

東方曾有好幾個世紀認為自己最優越。在這好幾個世紀裡，東方的子民大多足不出戶。畢竟，既然已在*世界的中心*，又何必探索遠方？

同樣的，西方也抱著相同的優越感，有些仍堅持*不照做就閃開的*心態。

歷史告訴我們，東西方一直面對著兩股強大但對立的力量；我們一方面想維護既有的生活方式，一方面又必須順應不斷改變的局勢。這兩股力量經常相衝突，且在文化、社會與經濟上有所分歧。

除非我們相互學習，瞭解彼此差異所帶來的益處，並珍惜共有的價值，否則東方或西方引領世界的時間都不會長久。

一條古老的巨物和一隻有創業精神的鳥，真的能幫我們促進相互的認識嗎？欲知結果…請待下回龍與鵬的對話…

Let's remember these words and reinforce them in our future meetings, Eagle. The speed of change won't allow either of us to sit and watch. You must regain your hunger for pioneering, while we must satisfy our hunger, while not overeating or becoming slothful.

You must move from a society of consumers, to a society of producers. And we must move from a society of manufacturers, to a society of creative and technological innovators.

We both must be patient *with one another,* but always impatient with ourselves or our achievements. We must be ready, at a moment's notice, to modify our approaches and procedures, keeping in mind our ancient proverb...*yuan shui jiu bu liao jin huo...a slow remedy will never meet an emergency.*

*(rising into the sky and thinking out loud)* The "have nots" must have full access to the knowledge to gain what the "haves" own. One thing is certain: knowledge and action govern both our futures.

As the Eagle disappeared among the clouds, the Dragon slowly slipped back into the enormous crack in the earth, where it contemplated the distant past and reviewed the promise for an even better future. Any Eagle who thinks the Dragon is hibernating does so at its own peril.The Dragon is anything but asleep. It's not even weary.

For centuries the East considered itself superior to all peoples with which it came in contact. Its citizens remained at home for the most part throughout the many centuries. After all, when you're the *center of the earth* why venture to far away lands?

In similar fashion, the West has maintained an equally superior attitude: *It's my way or the highway,* some continue to insist.

Historically, we all are confronting two powerful, opposing forces: the protection of our way of life and the acceptance of constant change—often colliding, repeatedly at odds culturally, socially and economically.

Unless we learn from each other, and understand the merits of our differences, while nurturing the values we have in common, neither East or West will dominate the world stage for long.

Could it be that a mighty, ancient creature and an enterprising bird may, in fact, provide us with further clues on achieving mutual understanding? We will see...as our dialogue between the Dragon and Eagle unfolds...

# 摘要

## 第二回

# Summary

## CHAPTER 2

# 一(不)如往常

# Business (Not) As Usual

# 龍親口告訴我們…

# *Straight from the Dragon's mouth...*

☯ 吃不只是為身體攝取營養而已。大宴賓客可幫助我們觀察未來生意伙伴的舉止。*參加我們的宴席時要小心，因為涉及的絕不只是北平烤鴨而已！*

☯ 西方必須更用心地與東方建立長期互動關係，不要只顧著找生意伙伴而已。*再用心些！*

☯ Eating is so much more than nourishment for the body. Feasts and banquets help us take stock of the behavior of future business associates. *Be on your guard when you attend one of our feasts, because there's more involved than Peking duck!*

☯ The West must focus more on developing long-term interaction with the East than simply looking for business contacts. *Work harder at this.*

# 鵬的看法則是…
# *From the Eagle's point of view...*

* 總之，與東方的事業伙伴發展長期關係時，持之以恆總是值得的，就算得喝好幾公升的茶也在所不惜。

* 西方能夠快速成功，基礎在「雙贏」的觀念。雙方都得贏，成就才能持久。我們的理念是：「對雙方都不公平的話，不做也罷。」

* In the end, it is always worth the effort to practice persistence when developing long-term relationships with business associates in the East—even when it means drinking gallons of tea.

* The rapid success of the West has been based on the concept of "win-win." We both must win in order for success to be lasting. Our philosophy is "if it isn't fair to both of us, we shouldn't do it."

# 龍親口告訴我們…

# *Straight from the Dragon's mouth...*

☯ 來這兒的外國朋友過於樂觀，過於相信別人，但耐心不足。別人贏的時候，我們常誤以為有人非輸不可。你們的雙贏觀念，我們必將實踐，只是時機未到而已。*鵰族的朋友，請發揮耐心。*

☯ 我們的文化，正快速地從「壓抑致富」轉型為「鼓勵致富」，從等公家給的社會，轉型為自己闖的社會。西方必須瞭解這就是我們的年輕人為什麼突然亟欲有所表現，出人頭地。

☯ Foreigners who come here often have too much optimism, too much trust and too little patience. For someone to win with us, we often operate under the faulty assumption that someone must lose. Your win-win concept is what we need to implement—and ultimately will—but not just yet. *Be patient with us, Eagles.*

☯ Our culture is moving rapidly from "wealth discouragement" to "wealth encouragement," and from an entitlement society to an entrepreneurial society. The West must be aware this is why our young people are suddenly hungry to make their individual marks and stand out among the masses.

# 鵬的看法則是…

# From the Eagle's point of view...

✶ 西方具備絕佳的經營模型，有些已開始在東方的情境下實踐。然而，西方須持續設計效能更佳的事業架構，以面對東方商業環境的巨大改變。

✶ *關係*這個詞，西方得再好好研究，這點龍已經說服我了。因此，在與高層的聯繫方面，東西方都必須避免把事業放在不靠某人，就得不到官方青睐的位置上。

✶ The West has excellent business models that it already implements in an Eastern context. However, it must continually design even more effective business frameworks to handle the sweeping changes in the East's commercial environment.

✶ The Dragon has convinced me that the West needs to have a better understanding of the word *guanxi*. Therefore, for connections in high places, it's prudent that neither East nor West put our businesses in a position where we are dependent on one individual for access to official blessings.

# 龍親口告訴我們…
# Straight from the Dragon's mouth...

☯ 有鑑於「國營企業」正轉型為「私營企業」，我們對創新的創投資金瞭解不深，運用也不足。由於我們封閉太久，因此真正的挑戰，在於更有效地吸收新觀點。正是在這方面，我們需要鵰的協助。

☯ With the transition from government-sponsored businesses to privately-owned businesses, we lag behind in our understanding and employment of creative venture capitalism. Also, we've lived inwardly for so long that our real challenge is to network more effectively with other points of view. This is where we need help from the Eagles.

## 鵬的看法則是…

# From the Eagle's point of view...

✶ 然而，我們的確需要熟知語言、文化與商務禮儀的合夥人或顧問，才能成功。

✶ 東方的經營模型種類繁多，若欲重整，西方可提供許多協助，在加深海外創投與國際貿易的知識上尤其如此。

✶ However, we do need business partners or consultants with excellent knowledge of language, culture and business etiquette to be successful.

✶ The West has much to offer the East to help it re-frame its wide-ranging business models—particularly in the areas of overseas venture capitalism and a deeper understanding of the world of international trade.

第三回

CHAPTER 3

# 重視品德

# Character Counts

**龍**與鵰現在知道每次他們在大岩縫的邊緣交談時，內容一定很精彩。鵰的話有什麼價值，龍一開始很難看出。龍畢竟幾千歲了，身上的鱗就可證明一切。龍也相信光他忘記的東西，就已經比鵰懂得的還多。

鵰也是一樣，有時邊飛邊咕噥著：「*龍活了很久沒錯，也很有智慧，但今天這個世界究竟什麼才重要，他又知道多少？下次見面一定要探個仔細。*」

每次空中傳來強大雙翼揮舞的聲音時，龍就慢慢抬頭看是不是鵰來了。若不是，龍居然會感到失望。或許龍很期待這位新朋友的到訪，只是不願承認而已。然而，這天下午雖然已經晚了，烈日仍把古老的東方照得發燙，此時鵰突然從天急降，且落地方式非誇張兩字不足以形容，龍盯得連心都少跳了一下，

午安，龍兄。您的氣色不錯，看起來雖然有點兒老，但老當益壯。

鵰兄，在東方，年紀大是種榮耀，是受到我們珍惜的，且程度應該超過西方。活得久有很多好處。我可能動作不像以前那麼快，但過去的朝代、戰爭和勝利，以及從古到今先師們的智慧與教誨，我可是記得一清二楚。鵰兄，您到了我這把年紀的時候，一定會下這個結論：長壽的目的在於培養品德。品德才是關鍵，而且造假不了。

By now, each time the Dragon and the Eagle met at the rim of the great crevice in the earth both knew the conversation would be stimulating indeed. It wasn't easy at first for the Dragon to see the value in all that the Eagle had to say. After all, the Dragon was thousands of years old. It had the scales to prove it. It was also convinced it had forgotten more than the Eagle had ever known.

In like manner, the Eagle would sometimes fly away muttering to itself, *Dragon may have lived a long time—and it has a lot of wisdom—but I wonder how up to date it is on things that really matter in today's world. I'll find out the next time we're together.*

Each time the Dragon heard the sound of strong wings flapping in the sky it slowly lifted its head upward to see if it was the Eagle. When it wasn't, the Dragon was surprisingly disappointed. Perhaps it missed its new friend more than it was willing to admit. But late this afternoon as the sun continued to blister the ancient Eastern earth with its heat, the Dragon's heart skipped a beat as it watched the Eagle come soaring in for what could only be described as a theatric landing.

Good afternoon, Dragon. You're looking well. Rather ancient today, I must admit, but healthy indeed.

In the East, it's a great honor to be old, Eagle. Age is something we cherish. Perhaps more than in the West. A prolonged existence has many virtues. I may not be able to move as quickly as I once moved, but my brain remembers all too well dynasties past, wars fought, battles won, and the wisdom of philosophers and their teachings from ancient times to today. When you're as old as I am, Eagle, you come to one conclusion: longevity is designed to produce character. Character is what matters, and character cannot be counterfeited.

龍兄，您說的我們再同意不過。我們可能沒法活得像您這麼久，累積這麼多智慧，但品德也是西方致力追求的。龍兄，我說個故事，這樣您會比較瞭解我的意思。

在西方某間著名大醫院的開刀房裡，有位護士第一天上班，負責的工作即將結束。「醫師，您只拿出十一塊紗布，」他對醫生說：「我們用了十二塊。」

「全拿出來了，」醫生反駁：「現在可以縫合了。」

「不行，」護士反對：「我們用了十二塊紗布。」

「我負全責，」醫生嚴厲地說：「縫！」

「不行！」護士說：「這樣病人怎麼辦？」

醫生微笑著把腳挪開，讓護士看見第十二塊紗布，然後說：「妳沒問題。」

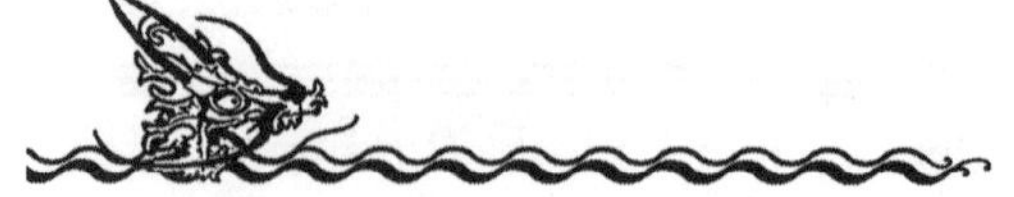

鵰兄，這故事我喜歡。原來鵰不需要幾千年的時間，就能培養品德。可是，培養品德需要自律、正直和…

…高度的自我尊重。有件事我不知東方會怎麼做，甚至做不做。在西方啊，為求不忘記尊重自己，我們可能會每天告訴自己：

✶ 天生我才必有用。內在價值是天生的，不須向外爭取。

✶ 我的挑戰，就是提升並保護我的價值。我絕對不讓這個為求成功不計代價的社會剝奪或扭曲我的價值

On that point we certainly agree, Dragon. We may not be as old as you or always as wise as you, but character is also a dominant desire among most people in the West. Dragon, let me tell you a story that says it better than I can.

In the operating room of a large, well-known hospital in the West, a young nurse was completing her first day of full responsibility. "You've only removed 11 sponges, Doctor," she said to the surgeon. "We used 12."

"I removed them all," the doctor declared. "We'll close the incision now."

"No," objected the nurse. "We used 12 sponges."

"I'll take the responsibility," the surgeon said grimly. "Suture!"

"You can't do that!" said the nurse. "Think of the patient."

The surgeon smiled, lifted his foot, and showed the nurse the twelfth sponge. "You'll do, he said."

I like that story, Eagle. Maybe Eagles don't have to be thousands of years old to develop character after all. But it does take constant discipline and integrity, and...

...and a personal code of deep self-respect. I don't know how people in East might do this—or even if they do—but individuals in my part of the world might recite their daily "self-respect" affirmations something like this:

✱ I am valuable because I've been created with inner value. I didn't have to earn it.

✱ My challenge is to nurture and protect my value. I simply must keep it from getting jaded or twisted by the values of a success-at-any-cost-oriented society.

✶ 我的價值在於我的承諾。我不怕承諾，而且說到做到。

✶ 我會對他人說：你我都有價值。我們可以交換價值。我把我最好的給你，也相信你會把最好的給我。

鵰兄，您今天有備而來，對不對？您還真是個哲學家，比實際年齡成熟多了。老實說，我對您刮目相看。我想在品德這個議題上，我們的看法頗為一致。可是，自認價值低落或看不起自己者，一定不接受我們這一套。這樣的行為準則，甚至說不定令他們感到厭惡。其他龍與鵰重視外在的肯定與操縱，並忽視內在的自尊時，這種現象就會發生。我擔心東方許多朋友目前就是如此。

龍讚美鵰展現出超齡的智慧時，鵰暗地裡高興極了，但他當然只眨眼點頭示意，假裝龍的讚美不算什麼。

鵰知道龍是十二生肖裡最吉祥的，且龍所象徵的一切，對東方而言至為重要。因此，鵰知道近代中國最傑出的人物之一鄧小平屬龍時，一點都不訝異。鵰甚至發現偶像李小龍的電影*龍爭虎鬥*是多麼重要。這位演員暨武術專家原來也屬龍。

龍兄，我剛才說護士的故事時，並沒有西方人全都品德高尚的意思。不過，這是大家追求的理想，但對我們這個崇拜名人的社會

✱ My worth is my word. I make commitments, and I do what I promise I say I'll do.

✱ I say to others: I am valuable, as you are valuable. Let us make a value exchange. I will offer you the best I have, and I assume you will give me your best in return.

Eagle, you certainly came prepared today, didn't you? You're really quite a philosopher. And even wise beyond your years—which actually surprises me. I don't think we're in much disagreement on this subject. But people who see little or no value in themselves will choose not to operate according to such a code. In fact, such a system of conduct might even be distasteful to them. This is what happens when other Dragons and Eagles become more concerned with outward recognition and manipulation than from a concern for self-respect. I fear this is what's happening to many people in the East today.

When the Dragon complimented the Eagle for expressing wisdom beyond its years, the Eagle quietly fluttered its wings, blinked an eye and nodded knowingly while, of course, pretending the Dragon's praise didn't matter at all.

The Eagle knew the Dragon was the most auspicious of all creatures of the zodiac, and that it held enormous significance as a symbol for what was important in the East. It was therefore no surprise to the Eagle that one of the most outstanding figures in China's contemporary history—Deng Xiaoping—was born in the Year of the Dragon. The Eagle had even discovered the importance of Bruce Lee's cult movie *Enter the Dragon.* He later learned that this actor/martial arts expert was also a Dragon.

Dragon, when I told you that story of the nurse earlier, I didn't mean to imply that everyone in the West maintains that kind of character. But we do strive for it. However, it's not easy in our

來說，很不容易。今天只要能擠到聚光燈下，就算只*爆紅一刻鐘*也好，就可能帶來大筆鈔票和出書機會，或者有機會巡迴演說，成為紀實劇情片的主角。我認為這對品德的培養有害無益。雖然東方向西方學到很多，但我擔心你們也吸收了一些最壞的部分。

鵰兄，您說的恐怕沒錯。在太平洋的此岸，有太多朋友越來越相信為求成功可以不惜一切。鵰兄，這點您或許可幫個忙。

這麼說好了，東方越來越有信心，渴望成為「世界公民」，但許多掌權者還是疑神疑鬼，對外面的世界感到恐懼。這就是為什麼大部分還是狹隘地以自我為中心，注意力幾乎都放在金錢上，而忽略了「非我族類」。

環境就是個例子。環境都快毀了，但大筆鈔票的聲音，還是比最迫切的環境問題好聽。天空受污染的程度，已經讓我們難以呼吸。富有的煙草工業簡直是在經營集中營。我們的人口佔全球的兩成，抽的香菸卻佔全球的三成，而且還是最大的香菸生產國。怎麼會這樣？*因為這個產業最賺錢！*

龍兄，到底是什麼原因，造成我們這樣魯莽地自我毀滅？不就是道德和內在價值的敗壞嗎？你們擁有經得起時間考驗的傳統，我們也有。西方文明的根基，大多建立在明確且絕對的道德觀上，而非視情況而定的道德觀上。可是現在，我們變得只想*做痛快的事*，而不是*做該做的事*。不論是個體或企業，不誠實的情況都非常普遍。龍兄，這讓我很擔心。

celebrity-obsessed culture. A few moments in the limelight—*15 minutes of instant fame*—can lead to big bucks, a book contract, a speaking tour or a TV docudrama. I see this as character-destroying rather than character-building. While the East has learned much from the West, my concern is that you've also absorbed some of our worst.

I'm afraid you're right, Eagle. Too many on this side of the great ocean support the increasingly popular belief that success at all costs is the only thing that matters. Maybe you can help us here, Eagle.

You see, while many in the East are becoming more self-confident and eager to become "world citizens," many in power are still paranoid and fearful of the outside world. That's why so many remain parochial, self-centered, and focus so much on money alone—not relationships with those "outside the clan."

One example is the environment. It's going up in smoke, and vast sums of money talk louder than the most critical environmental concern. Our skies are becoming so polluted that we cannot breathe. The already wealthy tobacco industry is running a death camp among our people. We are home to 20 percent of the world's population and yet we consume 30 percent of the world's cigarettes. We are now the largest producer of cigarettes in the world. Why? *That's where the money is!*

What is the cause, Dragon, of our mutual headlong pursuit of self-destruction? Is it not a bankruptcy of morals and inner values? You have your time-tested traditions and so do we. In the West, our civilization at large has been rooted in clearly defined moral absolutes, rather than on situational ethics. Now, we've morphed into a people who seem to want *to do what feels good* rather than *to do the right thing*. Personal and corporate dishonesty is rampant. This is of great concern to me, Dragon.

鵬兄，我們一定不能灰心喪氣。你們在西方是怎麼說的⋯*杯子是半滿，不是半空*？情況還沒到全盤皆輸的地步。我們的社會，不管是哪個階層，欺騙和貪腐的情況也非常普遍。可是，據我對一般民眾的觀察，我發現貪腐越嚴重，追求道德的慾望也越強。

舉個例子，有位住在沿海大城裡的老先生，最近驕傲地宣布有天晚上他撿到一個皮夾，裡面有很多錢。*第二天早上，這位先生把皮夾和錢全數歸還原主*。

鵬兄，還有呢。在東方，見多識廣的*計程車司機*，非常重視禮儀。有位司機說若客人要去宗教場所，就不收車錢，*因為這些人是好人，從不說髒話，也絕不隨便罵人*。我的意思，不是要有宗教信仰或燒香拜佛才算好人，但宗教似乎幫得上忙。

龍兄，我擔心西方在坐吃山空。那些經得起時間考驗的道德傳統，正在快速瓦解中。最能反映文化現況的，莫過於年輕人的習慣。我們的統計數字美化不了：青少年懷孕的比例正在上升。在西方某個國家，酒醉駕車導致的交通事故，每十五秒就發生一次，每廿三分鐘就有一個兒童死於車禍，而且通常跟酒精或毒品脫不了關係。

東方也有類似的問題，且我們如果跟著你們的文化腳步走，情況只會更為惡化。可是，對品格和正直的追求，也一樣從未中斷。你們有份高品質的報紙*紐約時報*，曾報導過這麼一個消息。某著名的網路佈告板，公告某位先生譴責某疑似跟他太太發生外遇的大學生。

But we must not be discouraged, Eagle. How do you say it in the West...about *seeing the glass half full rather than half empty?* All is not lost. Yes, we, too, are plagued with dishonesty and corruption at all levels in our society. However, as I survey the common people from my vantage point, I sense that when corruption increases so does the desire for ethical behavior.

For example, an elderly person in one of our great coastal cities recently proudly announced that one night he'd found a wallet containing a great deal of money. *The gentleman returned it to its rightful owner the next morning—money and all.*

Something else, Eagle. Civility ranks high in the East among those who have heard and seen it all—*our taxi drivers.* One cab driver says he doesn't charge people a fare if they ask to be taken to a place of worship...*"this is because they are nice people who treat me with kindness. They never swear. They never bawl me out."* I'm not saying an individual must have faith in the gods or bow and burn incense to be a good person, but it does seem to help.

Dragon, in the West I fear we are living on past capital. Our time-tested ethical traditions are fast eroding. And nothing shouts louder about a culture's condition than the habits of its youths. Our record needs no embellishing: our teenage pregnancy is on the rise. Every fifteen seconds, in one of our countries, a traffic accident involving a drunk driver takes place. In that same nation, every twenty-three minutes a child dies in an automobile crash, usually where alcohol or other drugs are involved.

The East has similar problems, only on a larger scale if we follow in your cultural footsteps. But again, the pursuit of character and integrity is alive. One of your great newspapers, *The New York Times,* wrote of one such incident. Apparently a popular Internet

數百位網友立刻加入撻伐行列。有個人是這麼寫的…*讓我們用鍵盤和滑鼠把這些通姦者的頭砍下來，好彌補那位先生做出的犧牲*。幾天之內，幾百人變成幾千人，然後幾萬人，連陌生人都組織起來，試圖揪出那名大學生，把他趕出學校，逼得他的家人不敢踏出家門。

嗯*（笑）*，這跟所有其它沒人注意的不公不義相比，好像有點太嚴厲了。可是，看來我們還是有希望的，龍兄。我可以想像那個學生逃命的樣子。可是，如果我們希望這樣的道德感成為核心價值，就必須做誠實正直的榜樣給孩子看。沒這種正面影響的話，我們就真要為東西方的未來感到憂心了。

嘿，龍兄，我飛回西方之前，可以讀一首我最近看到的詩給您聽嗎？我覺得這首詩可以做為今天談話的總結。

當然可以。您也知道東方對詩的愛好。鵰兄，這首詩的主題是什麼？

人格與正直的重要性，以及在眾人前身體力行的必要性。名為*聽聽孩子的話*…

bulletin board told of a husband who denounced a college student he suspected of having an affair with his wife. Immediately, hundreds of Internet visitors joined in the attack. One person wrote something like...*Let us use our keyboard and mouse as weapons to chop off the heads of these adulterers, to pay for the sacrifice of the husband.* Within days, apparently the hundreds had grown to thousands, and then to tens of thousands, with complete strangers forming teams that chased down the student, hounded him out of his university and forced his family to barricade themselves inside their home.

Well, *(laughing)* that seems a little harsh compared to all the other injustices in society that get little attention. But, I guess there's hope for us after all, Dragon. I can still see that student running for his life. If we want to see that kind of morality be a core value, however, we must live lives of truth and integrity in front of our children. Without that positive influence, we will have justifiable fears for the futures of both East and West.

Say, Dragon, before I fly back to the West today, may I read you a poem I came across recently? I think it sums up much of what we've been saying.

Of course. You know how we in the East enjoy poetry. What's the subject of the poem, Eagle?

It's about the importance of character and integrity, and how vital it is to model these qualities for others. It's entitled *Listen to the Children...*

*今天，花點時間*

*聽聽孩子說什麼*

*無論如何，聽一聽*

*否則他們以後不聽你的*

*聽他們的問題，聽他們的需要*

*贏得再少，要讚美，做得再少，要讚美*

*他們話多時，要容忍，他們歡笑時，要加入*

*關心他們怎麼了，關心他們要什麼*

*每晚，都要說你多愛他們*

*罵他們，也要抱他們*

*告訴他們一切都沒關係*

*若我們說的，是他們的缺點*

*他們長大後，就滿是缺失*

*若我們說的，是父母的驕傲*

*他們長大後，就必然勝利*

*今天，花點時間*

*聽聽孩子的話*

*無論如何，聽一聽*

*他們以後就聽你的！*

*Take a moment to listen today*
*To what your children are trying to say*

*Listen today, whatever you do*
*Or they won't be there to listen to you*

*Listen to their problems, listen for their needs*
*Praise their smallest triumphs, praise their smallest deeds*

*Tolerate their chatter, amplify their laughter*
*Find out what's the matter, find out what they're after*

*But tell them that you love them, every single night*
*And though you scold them, make sure you hold them,*
*And tell them Everything's all right.*

*If we tell our children all the bad in them we see*
*They'll grow up exactly how we hoped they'd never be*
*But if we tell our children, we're so proud to wear their name*
*They'll grow up believing they're winners in the game.*

*Take a moment to listen today*
*To what your children are trying to say*
*Listen today, whatever you do*
*And they will come back to listen to you!*

「*他們以後就聽你的！*」這句話還迴盪在巨大的岩縫中時，鵬已揮動著巨大的雙翼，朝西方的巢歸去。

龍從胸膛深處發出隆隆的低吼，以表達對鵬剛說的話是多麼認同。龍帶著他特有的微笑，緩慢而仔細地轉動身軀。就在同時，他注意到一群幼龍在身後玩耍。他們顯然剛才一直都在他的腳下。龍之前根本沒注意到。這個東方智慧與力量的奇麗象徵停了一下，發現自己突然能從全新的角度觀察幼龍。然後，他用只有自己才聽得見的聲音吟著⋯

*今天，花點時間*

*聽聽孩子的話*

*無論如何，聽一聽*

*他們以後就聽你的！*

While the words *"and they will come back to listen to you"* reverberated from the massive walls within the great fissure in the earth, the Eagle lifted its mighty wings and flew back to its home in the West.

The Dragon let go with a mighty rumble from deep within its chest, apparently its way of indicating it approved of what it had just heard from the Eagle. Smiling as only Dragons can, it turned its massive body slowly and deliberately. As it did, it noticed a group of smaller Dragons playing a game behind him. They had apparently been at his feet the entire time. The Dragon simply hadn't paid attention. The breathtaking symbol of Eastern wisdom and power paused for a moment, looking at the smaller Dragons suddenly with new eyes. Then, in a voice heard only by itself, it intoned the words…

*Take a moment to listen today*
*To what your children are trying to say*
*Listen today, whatever you do*
*And they will come back to listen to you!*

## 摘要

第三回

## Summary

CHAPTER 3

# 重視品德

# Character Counts

# 龍親口告訴我們…

# Straight from the Dragon's mouth...

☯ 長壽在東方是受到推崇與尊敬的。***千萬別忘記這點！***

☯ 精彩人生所能帶來的最佳價值，就是品德。品德不容忽視，且無法造假。***別當個冒牌貨。***

☯ 人們比較在意外界的肯定，而非自我的尊重，並非個人或國家之福。***同心協力才能力挽狂瀾。***

☯ In the East, a long life is to be honored and respected. ***Don't forget it!***

☯ The greatest quality to be gained through a life well lived is character. Character matters. Character cannot be counterfeited. ***Don't be a phony.***

☯ When people are more concerned with outward recognition than with their own self-respect, the result is not in the best interest of the individual or the nation. ***Be the power of one to help turn the tide.***

## 鵰的看法則是…

# From the Eagle's point of view...

✭ 西方相信最好的表現，可強化個人對自我的尊重…意即*我是有價值的；我的價值反映在我的承諾上。我說到做到。*

✭ 為求出名不惜一切的文化，可能使人爆紅爆富。然而，到最後可能造成的，是品德的淪落，而非提升。*慢慢來。簡單就好。腳踏實地。*

✭ 道德與內在價值觀的淪喪，會導致敗亡。若不發揮智慧調整方向，自我毀滅在所難免。*您現在有什麼貢獻？*

✭ In the West, when at our best, we affirm a personal code of self-respect that says...*I am valuable; my worth is my word. What I promise I will do.*

✭ Our celebrity-obsessed culture may lead to big money and instant fame. However, in the end this may be more character-destroying than character-building. *Slow down. Keep it simple. Be real.*

✭ A bankruptcy in morality and inner values will be our doom. We are wise to alter our course, or face self-destruction. *What are you doing to make a difference?*

# 龍親口告訴我們…

# *Straight from the Dragon's mouth...*

☯ 在地球的這一端，「金錢」仍然比環境議題還重要。繼續下去的話，則危險自負。***全力保護老天所賜。***

☯ 若我們留意今天的警訊，就有希望共同擁有美好的明天。每個欺騙的行為，似乎總有一股追求真相的慾望與之抗衡。***問問東西方的計程車司機，就知道啦！***

☯ On this side of the great ocean, "talking money" continues to take precedence over environmental concerns. If this continues, it is to our peril. ***Do your part to protect what we've been given.***

☯ There is hope for our better future together if we heed the warning signs today. For every act of dishonesty, there always seems to be an equal desire for truth. ***Ask the cab drivers in both the East and the West. They'll tell you!***

## 鵰的看法則是…

# *From the Eagle's point of view...*

✯ 西方似乎在坐吃山空。未來看重的，應該是人格與責任。*一切從現在開始！*

✯ 聆聽孩子的話。聆聽他們的問題。用口頭表達您對他們的愛。*無論如何，聽一聽…他們以後就聽您的！*

*您真的在聽嗎？*

✯ The West seems to be living off its past capital. The new currency must be the pursuit of integrity and responsibility. *Do it now!*

✯ Listen to the children. Listen to their problems. Tell them you love them. *Listen today, whatever you do...and they will come back to listen to you.*

*Are you listening?*

第四回

CHAPTER 4

# 家庭第一

# Family First

鵬與龍雖然幾天沒見，但你幾乎聽得見他們的大腦在轉個不停，思考下次要談什麼。

可以談的這麼多，在文化與人民上，可相互學習的地方也這麼多。很神奇的，是鵬與龍彷彿有心電感應，都決定下一個主題，應該是東方與西方的家庭觀。

綜觀歷史，凡是安全且穩定的社會，還有哪一個機制比家庭還重要？

鵬迫不及待地想開始分享，於是決定再次飛越大岩縫後就落地。龍也很想開始，於是眨了眨他老邁的眼睛，把身軀挪動到一個比較舒服的姿勢，以迎接他的好朋友。

鵬兄，早安。很高興咱們又見面了。我們談過的，再加上這麼多還沒談的，讓我的思路整個活絡起來。我們最好趁早開始。您也知道，再拖我就更老了。

別這麼說，龍兄。我看您應該會長生不老，至少我這麼希望。我對東方的理解加深了許多。老實說，與您交談是我這輩子最神奇的經驗。認識您之前，我真的以為大多數的問題，我都已經有答案了。現在我才知道我不懂的還真多。咱們開始吧。

我們先談談東西方的家庭觀，您說怎麼樣？

Even though the Eagle and the Dragon had been apart for several days, you could almost hear the wheels in their brains turning as each pondered what the next subject of their dialog might be.

There was still so much to discuss, so much to learn about each other's cultures and people. Strangely, in a telepathic way, both the Eagle and Dragon determined in their minds that the next order of business would be the family as viewed by both East and West.

Is it not true that throughout history there has never been a secure and stable human society in which any institution has been more important than the family?

Eager to contribute to the conversation, the Eagle made its final pass over the great crack in the earth. With a wink in one of its ancient eyes, the Dragon, also eager to talk, moved its body into a more comfortable position to welcome its Eagle friend.

Good morning, Eagle. It's good to see you. You've got my brain working in a thousand different directions. Not only because of what we've already discussed, but because we still have so much more ground to cover. So we'd better move quickly. I'm not getting any younger, you know.

My Dragon friend, come on. You'll probably live forever. Or at least I hope so. I'm learning so much about the East. In fact, being with you is one of the most amazing experiences of my life. I honestly thought I had answers to most of my questions before I met you. Now, I'm starting to realize how much I don't know. So let the dialogue begin.

And shall we start today by talking about how the East and West view the institution of the family?

龍兄，我正好也這麼想。既然您說我沒耐性、熱過頭且總想搶第一，我就先靜靜地坐在樹枝上仔細聽。

鵬兄，您真客氣。好吧，我先開始。根據東方的傳統智慧，家庭總是有三代、四代甚至五代同堂。幾個世紀來都是如此。有位過去的東方哲學家，一直提醒我們子女應孝順父母，且要在大家庭裡一*脈相傳*。儘管這不是什麼明文規定，但只有在極特殊的情況下，才可以違反這個原則。此一家庭模式多年來幾經調整，，但「顧家」的觀念並未完全改變。當然，家庭關係的某些轉變，是我不太同意的。

可是，龍兄，東方家庭實際上已改變了多少？

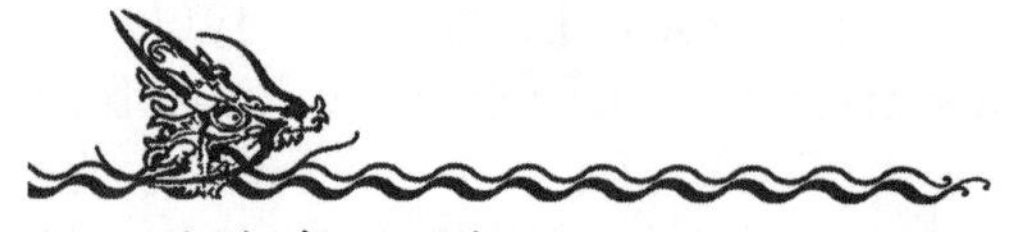

好，雖然我不太想承認，但不瞞您說，今天社會普遍追求的，已逐漸變成愛情與金錢，而不是敬老。約會談戀愛才是主流，跟父母和祖父母同住已經逐漸式微了。

My thoughts exactly, Dragon. Since you say I am often impatient, overly eager, and always wanting to jump into things headfirst, I'm going to sit here quietly on my perch and listen attentively.

How kind of you, Eagle. All right, I'll begin. In the East, it is conventional wisdom that our families have always been composed of three, four—even five—generations living under one roof. This has been standard procedure for centuries. One of the East's former great philosophers always reminded us that children were, by unwritten law, expected to care for their parents in an *unbroken line* in an extended family setting. Only extreme circumstances would allow for the violation of this principle. While this family model been has been modified over the years, the idea of "taking care of members of the family" has not completely changed. Although, there are shifts in family relationships I don't much approve of.

But, in reality, Dragon, how much has the family in the East really changed?

Okay, I'll be honest. Although it's hard for me to admit it. The all-pervasive dynamic today is gradually becoming more about love and money than respecting our elders. Dating and falling in love are in vogue; living under the same roof with parents and grandparents is becoming passé.

龍兄，這一定都不好嗎？我知道這跟你們的悠久傳統相差很遠，但這代表社會走錯方向了嗎？畢竟，西方長久多年來都是如此。關鍵在於自立。對我們來說，度蜜月讓夫妻在實質上切斷他們與家庭之間的臍帶。新娘和新郎其實在告訴大家：*好，各位，我們自立了。偶爾來看看我們可以，但從現在開始，我們要自己作主了，謝謝！*

有趣。我們也發現如今年輕夫妻選擇與老人家「保持距離」。他們就是越來越不想同堂。

可是鵰兄您別誤解。家庭對我們來說還是很重要。我們不願意像你們一樣，把無法照顧自己的老人送進養老院，除非他們需要全天候照護。我們覺得對老人家有責任，因為我們還是無助的嬰兒時，就是他們辛苦照顧的。

反正今天有些變化，是我無法接受或理解的，但再怎麼樣，我們做什麼事都還是以家庭為單位。我說過東方社會基本上較喜歡「待在家」，而不是四處闖，不知您記得嗎？。我們願意*在家裡與家人一起為家做事*。這種互信的感覺，似乎就是沒辦法與外人分享。我們真的信任家人。你們是怎麼說的？是不是雙面刃？重視家庭是我們的長處，也是短處。我們就是不想遠離這種既有的安全感。瞭解這一點，對你們到這兒經商應該有幫助。

And is that all bad, Dragon? I know it's a major departure from your long-held traditions, but does it mean your society is moving in the wrong direction? After all, this is where the West has been for years. Independence is the name of our game. For us the honeymoon is a physical event that "cuts the umbilical cord" between a couple and their families. It's a way for the bride and groom to say, *Okay, folks, we're now on our own. You can come visit us once in a while, but from now on we'll be making our own decisions, thank you!*

Interesting. We, too, are finding young married couples are choosing to live a "bowl of soup" away from their elders. More and more, they simply don't want to live under the same roof.

But Eagle, don't misunderstand me. Family is still critically important for us. We are uncomfortable with your practice of putting your old people, who can no longer care for themselves, in nursing homes unless they need constant attention. We feel obligated to our elders since they devoted themselves to us when we were helpless infants.

There are just some changes in the wind I don't like or understand. But the bottom line is that we still do everything as a family unit. Do you remember when I told you that the East was essentially a "stay at home" society more than a nation of internationalists? It's true. We work *with* our family, *within* the family and *for* the family. It seems we aren't always able to share that trust with outsiders. But we do trust family members. What do you call it—a two-edged sword? The family is both our strength and a weakness. But we just don't like to step away from our built-in security. This might be a helpful insight for when you do business with us.

沒錯，龍兄。東方社會的安定，顯然大多源自歷代以來對家庭的效忠。有段期間我們也是這樣。所有西方社會的起源都是鄉村，不是都市。以前，我們的孩子們會跟父母在農場裡幹活。日出而作，日落而息。家庭很重要。耕耘、播種與收割，都是全家一起來。

這種情況在我們這兒還是很普遍。近七成的人口以務農為生，許多的土地，不像你們一樣可以用機器耕作。要在全新的「知識時代」裡引領風潮，我們唯一的辦法，就是把龍從偏遠農村移至工業化的現代都市。我們正在執行一項計畫，讓至少六成的龍能盡快從農村遷移到都市。您可能也注意到了，全世界大多數的建材都是往這兒送。在未來十到十五年內，我們必須建立足夠的城市、大學和企業，來容納數量超越貴國的人口。

鵰兄，以前你們的拓荒者坐馬車向西遷移，有鑽油熱和淘金熱，還有人不斷地從農場移向工廠。可是，我們得在廿年內，把將近五億人從農村移至都市從事技術工作。您曾經想過我們要面對的規模嗎？

*（雙翼全展）*哇！我想西方根本無法想像這會對生活和文化造成什麼改變，以及需要哪些基礎建設。西方的遷移大概花了一百年，目前住在農村裡的人不到百分之五。

Indeed so, Dragon. It's apparent that much of the social stability of the East has been due to the allegiance to family for centuries of generations. For a period of time the situation was similar for us. All societies in the West began in rural, not urban, settings. In the past, our children worked the farms with their parents. They were all up at dawn and ceased their labors at sundown. Family was important. Together our families tilled the land, planted the crops and reaped the harvest.

This is still the case throughout much of Dragonland. Nearly 70 percent of our population survives by farming land, much of which is impossible to till with machines as you have done. The only way we can become leaders in the new "knowledge era" is to move our Dragons from rural farms to industrialized, modern cities. We are implementing a plan wherein at least 60 percent of our Dragons will move from rural to urban centers as expeditiously as possible. As you may have noticed, most of the world's building materials are being shipped here. During the next ten to fifteen years, we must build enough cities, universities, and businesses to accommodate more people than the population of your entire country.

Eagle, you had your settlers moving westward in wagons, you had your oil gushes, gold rushes and steady migration from farms to factories. But have you ever considered the magnitude of what we face in moving close to half a billion farmers into skilled jobs in cities in less than two decades?

*(opening its wings to their full spread)* Wow! I don't think anyone in the West has an inkling of what that means in terms of lifestyle and cultural change. And of the infrastructures you must put in place. Today, in the West, after that migration which took nearly a hundred years, we have less than 5 percent of our population living on farms.

*（微笑）*現在您知道我這條老龍移動腿的速度，要比您這年輕小伙子揮翅膀的速度快九倍才行。鵬兄，有件事讓我想不通，想請教一下。你們的孩子現在又不用在農忙時到田裡幫忙，為什麼夏天還是將近二個半月不用上學？

*（也微笑）*您的洞裡一定裝了衛星電視，對吧？沒想到您住這麼遠，觀察依舊敏銳。我們孩子休息的時間確實比上兩個世紀多。這是個問題，但從某些角度來看，又長又熱的夏天裡空閒時間太多，倒也有些好處。可是，我們先別談這個。我們既然喝了這麼多茶，如果能配上些糯米糕和零嘴，就可以再找個時間專門談這個問題。我也會帶點心來。您的藥草茶種類多，下次見面的時候，不妨挑些讓我嚐嚐。據我瞭解，這些茶有很多神秘療效！

我呢，當然很樂意向您介紹不同的茶。

這麼多世紀來，我們熟知各類天然營養和養生方法，這早就不是什麼秘密。看我就知道啦！我這把年紀，體格和精神都還算好吧？

若在西方，您可以上購物頻道或實境節目大賺一筆，向嬰兒潮出生的人示範怎麼對抗老化和地心引力。好，龍兄，我們別鬧了。

以前外在的干擾很少。沒有電視、廣播、手機、iPod™、電郵、DVD或其它媒體會影響合作的進行。很多時候，不止一代的家人會住在同個屋簷下，與東方的家庭非常類似。

*(smiling)* So you understand that the old Dragon has to move its legs ten times as fast as you have beat your wings throughout your brief history. And tell me something, Eagle, that has puzzled me. Why do your children still have no school for over two and a half months during the summer, when they no longer have to help their families with the seasonal cultivation on farms?

*(smiling back)* So you must have satellite TV in your cave, do you? You are very observant from such a distance. Yes, our children are idle much more than in the previous two centuries. This is a problem, but there are some positive aspects of having too much free time during the long, hot summers. But let's not discuss that now. It's worth another entire session, if we can add some rice cakes and munchies to the many cups of tea we've had together. I'll bring the sweets. Maybe in future meetings you can offer samples of your many different types of herbal teas. I understand they are full of secret health remedies!

Well, I'll be happy to introduce you to a variety of our teas.

It's no secret that we have learned much about natural nutrition and longevity through the centuries. Why, just look at me! Am I not strong and hearty for my age?

In the West, you could make a fortune doing an infomercial or reality TV show on how baby boomers can defy age and gravity. But let's get serious, Dragon.

There were few external distractions in the old days. No television, radio, cell phones, iPod™s, e-mail, DVDs, or other media to blunt the focus of working together. In many cases, more than one generation even lived under one roof, much like your families in the East.

可是，這種家庭凝聚在一起的情況，在西方幾乎已經絕跡。連一起吃飯都很難得了…

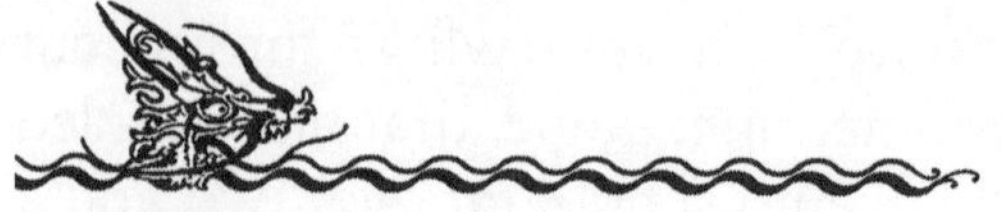

…這種情況在東方也越來越普遍。夫妻工作十二到十四小時，一星期六天，也只能勉強過日子而已。夫妻在工廠或辦公室加班到很晚，所以祖父母或親戚幫忙看孩子的情形很正常。在我們這兒沒什麼朝九晚五，有的應該是朝七晚十，而且星期一到星期六都上班。

有沒有托兒所？

只有高收入才付得起保母或專業托兒服務，但我們堅信不管什麼年齡的孩子，都須要大人管教。我們也有幼稚園和其它托育機構，但大多數都是由親戚幫忙。

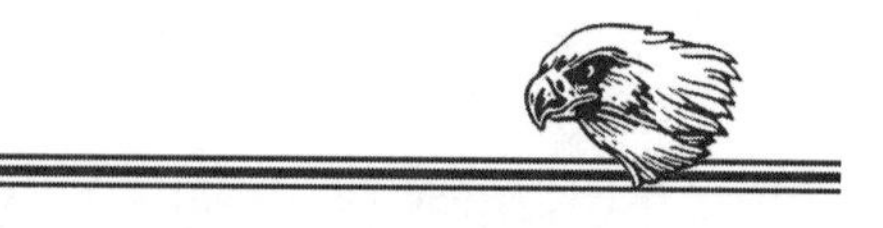

所以，孩子交給祖父母管教？

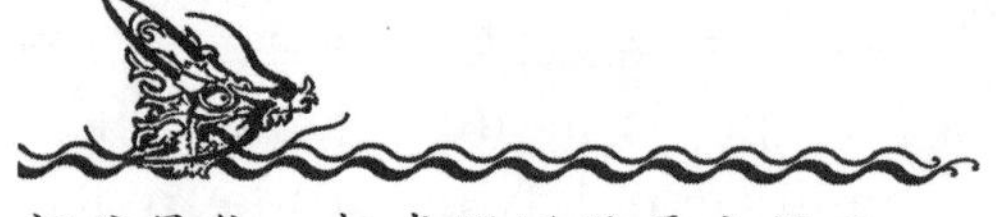

祖父母住一起或附近就更方便了。

孩子們晚上還經常回學校，在大人的看管下參加活動和做功課，好充實自己趕上西方！所以沒錯，我們的孩子用功讀書，但家人共處的時間卻不多了。

However, one would be hard-pressed to find hardly any situations today where the Western family maintains this kind of solidarity. Few families even eat together...

...and it's fast becoming that way in the East also. Husbands and wives both work 12- to 14-hour days, six days a week, to eke out a modest living. It is still common practice for grandparents and extended family members to supervise the young children, while their parents are in factories or offices well into the evening. There is no such thing as 9 to 5 in Dragonland. It is more like 7 a.m. to 10 p.m., Monday through Saturday.

Do you have day care centers?

Only the upper class can afford baby-sitters or professional child care, but we believe strongly in adult supervision for children of all ages. We do have pre-schools and other centers, but mostly extended family members are involved.

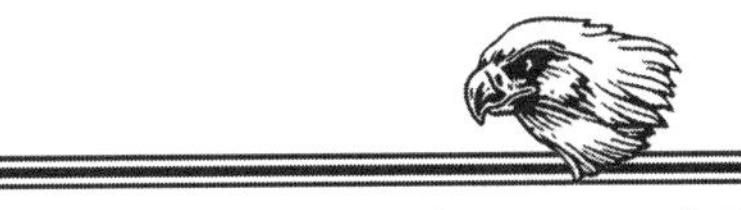

So the grandparents become the adult supervisors for your children?

It's easier if the grandparents live in the same place or nearby.

Our children often return back at school in the evenings, for supervised activities and to do their homework—trying to improve their minds to keep up with the advances of the West! So yes, our children further their education, but there isn't much family time anymore.

週末呢？

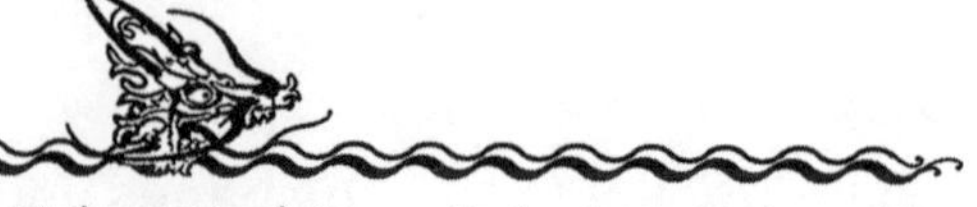

星期天的時候，你會看見全家人整天在一起放風箏玩遊戲，從古至今都沒改變。可是，父母和孩子星期天有時會分別參加研習會或其它訓練。所以，「家」這個長久以來受到珍惜的傳統，實際上恐怕在慢慢地消失中。

龍兄，歡迎加入現代世界。西方的晚餐時間，現在好像是賽車場裡的維修站，家人得輪流吃飯才行。吃飯時間以前是親子輕鬆交心，縮小代溝的最佳時機，但現在已不是常態，反而是例外。父親跟孩子溝通的時間，一星期不到一小時。

我們這兒的家庭也是一樣，只不過父親在星期天，會盡量把時間留給太太和孩子。

我對這樣的狀況不太滿意，但您曾經試過獨力扭轉情勢嗎？我們的確可以把這種發展，怪罪到很多事情上，像是雙薪才夠用、電視、互聯網、都市化、理念改變、愛錢愛權、忽視傳統價值觀、好萊塢和其它事情上，但是…

What about weekends?

On Sundays you will find families and their children spending the entire day together flying kites and playing games as we have done since ancient times. Some Sundays, however, are devoted to attending seminars and other training programs by parents and children separately. I fear, however, our long-cherished tradition of "family" is fading slowly but surely.

Dragon, welcome to the modern world. Dinner time in the West has become more like a "pit stop" at an auto race, where families eat in shifts. Meal time used to be the ideal time for the generation gap to be narrowed by open conversations between parents and children in a relaxed environment. This has become the exception, rather than the rule. Fathers spend less than an hour per week communicating with each of their children.

That's about the same in our families, only fathers devote most of their Sundays to be with wife and children.

I don't much like it either, but have you ever tried to reverse a trend single-handedly? I suppose we can blame these trends on the need for two income families, television, the Internet, urbanization, changing philosophies, love for money and power, movement away from old values, Hollywood and the rest, but...

…的確，找個東西怪或許不難。可是當一個社會只顧不計代價地賺錢、購物或手機不離耳，好像已經縫在上面的時候，最後一定會付出慘痛代價。這種矛盾令人不安。我們努力賺錢，為的是有更多空閒時間享受生活。*沒花時間照顧孩子*讓我們有罪惡感，所以我們*用花錢收買孩子*來補償。通常要到一切都太遲了，我們才知道孩子的愛不能用錢買，因為他們得到的是錢，不是時間，所以就把父母親看成「*深不見底的錢袋*」。

龍兄，千真萬確。沒有什麼能取代「親自」與孩子相處。

你們在電視上展現的西方文化，的確反映了這樣的衝擊，遠方的我們雖然看見了，但還是盲從，彷彿同意對生活水準的追求是進步，而不是愚昧。我們雙方都必須明辨「生活水準」和「生活品質」之間的差別。生活水準是你有多少錢可以花。生活品質是你決定如何利用那個珍貴但有限的資源，也就是時間。

龍兄，您說得真對。我們常把生活水準和生活品質搞混了，答案也並不簡單。龍族都是工作狂，我們鵰族卻忙著安排「舒壓」活動，而不是「奪標」活動，結果大家都成為「時間不足」的受害者。我們就像古羅馬人一樣，需要更多的金錢和感官刺激才能滿足。我們渴望看到競技場中的原始格鬥，但其實我們真正該做的，是為自己不安的靈魂尋找平靜，或者從事較振奮人心的活動，來讚頌生活及內在的美麗與創意。

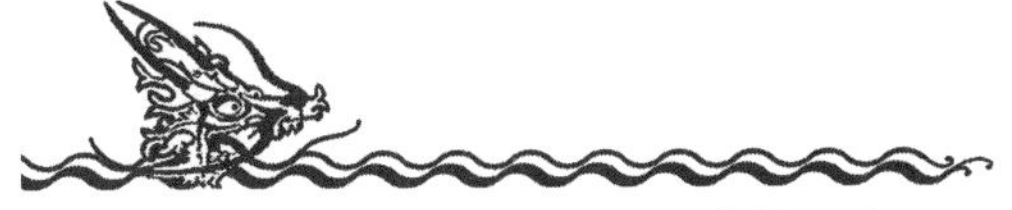

...yes, it's probably not difficult to assign blame. But when a society devotes all its effort to making money at all costs, buying goods, having a cell phone in its ear as if it were implanted, that society ultimately does so at great cost. It is a disquieting paradox. We work very hard to make more money so we can have more free time to enjoy life. Because we feel guilty about *not spending time with our children,* we try to compensate by *spending money on our children.* Only when it is too late do we realize that children's love cannot be purchased. Children, who are given money instead of time, view their parents as "bottomless pockets."

How true this is, Dragon. Nothing can replace "being there in person" with our children.

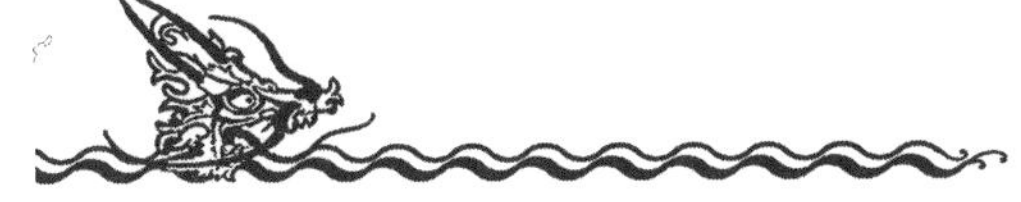

We see the impact of this as we view your Western culture on TV from a distance and yet we seem to follow you as if you were enlightened rather than blinded by your quest for standard of living. We both need to make a clear distinction between "standard of living" and "quality of life." Standard of living is how much money you have to spend. Quality of life is how you choose to spend that more precious, finite resource which we call TIME.

You're right, Dragon. We both have standard of living and quality of life all mixed up and the answers are not that simple. You Dragons are workaholics and we Eagles are so busy trying to fill up our calendars with "tension relieving" instead of "goal achieving" activities that we are suffering from "time starvation." And like the ancient Romans, we need more and more sensory stimulation to entertain ourselves. We hunger for more visceral action, in arenas and coliseums, when we should be seeking some quiet time to sooth our restless souls or more uplifting diversions that celebrate life, inner beauty and creativity.

在西方，老年化的人口驅動著經濟發展。在東方，驅動力量則是較年輕的一代。我們約有二億介於十五到廿四歲的小龍，且每年又會有二千萬幼龍進入青春期。

這代表著他們的手機與鈴聲比西方人口的總和還多！

這個趨勢所代表的，遠比聊天和噪音還令人擔憂。您也親眼目睹過了。年輕一代渴望有足夠的錢，好買最新的互聯網玩意兒、名牌服飾及其它富豪名流才有的象徵。正在脫離父母的青少年，迫不急待想得到成年榜樣才有的特權，卻不想負起相對應有的責任。

歡迎加入，原來你們也卡在「時尚」與「實力」間進退兩難。我們可是深陷其中，簡直快滅頂了。膚淺的糖衣取代了真正的自尊，也美化了年輕人浮躁的情緒。外表變得比我們對社會有什麼貢獻還重要。娛樂成為目的地，不再是旅途中的休息站而已。

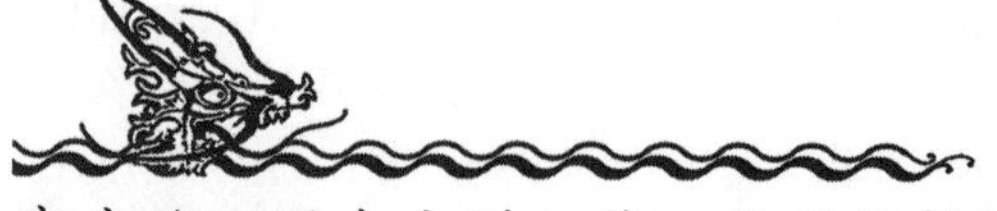

家庭的可用支出增加後，孩子就想用時髦、流行和無禮來表現自我。他們會想盡辦法並任意揮霍，以凸顯自己跟父母的不同。

In the West, your aging population has driven your economic trends. In the East, our younger population is the driving force. We have 200 million young Dragons between the ages of 15 and 24, and each year 20 million more adolescents reach puberty.

That translates into more cell phones and ringtones than people who live in the entire West!

It translates into something much more disturbing than chatter and noise. You've witnessed it yourself. The younger generation yearns for enough money to buy all the latest Internet-based gadgets, designer brands of clothing and accessories, and other trappings of the lifestyles of the rich and famous. As adolescents, breaking away from their parents, they desperately want the privileges of adult role models, without the responsibilities that must balance them.

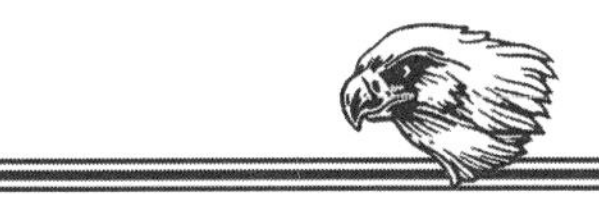

Welcome to the "style" over "substance" dilemma. We're mired in it up to our beaks, with no relief in sight. The emotional uncertainties of our youth are being sugar-coated by skin-deep substitutes for authentic self-esteem. How we look has become more important than what we have to offer in our contribution to society. Entertainment has become the destination, not simply a rest stop on the journey.

As our families have more spending money, our children want to express their individuality by being trendy, fashionable and irreverent. They spend a great effort and as much money as possible being different from their parents.

所以，西方和東方都應該及時清醒，否則就會重蹈過往帝國與王朝的盛衰。我們雖然有點遲了，但還有希望。如果我們能由家長帶頭展開草根運動，也許就能扭轉乾坤，再多撐幾個世紀。可是，龍兄您聽我說，你們的社會離走下坡也只差一步，而且致命的那一跌不用一世紀的時間。何況您剛剛才有智慧地說過，你們的經濟成長是如此快速，時間已經已被壓縮到以月計算，而不是以十年計算。

可是，與其在這兒擰著爪子自怨自艾，還不如談一些解決方法？您是行動快的鳥，眼光又銳利。我們別再模糊描述該做的事了。為求生存和繁榮，談談實際的作為怎麼樣？

好，首先，東方的父母會跟孩子「聊聊」嗎？

*（眉毛上揚）*您指的，是聊「嬰兒打哪兒來」這種尷尬的話題嗎？

*（猛搖頭）*不是，龍兄，不是那種，而是父母很少告訴孩子「樹上是不長錢的！」。錢是西方家庭最不常談的話題。父母似乎不想讓孩子知道有這麼多帳單要付，是多麼辛苦。

So both West and East must get a wake-up call now before we keep repeating the rise and fall of all empires and dynasties past. It's a little late in the game for us, but there's still hope. If we can begin a grass roots movement among family leaders, we may be able to defy the odds and hang around for a few more centuries. But listen to me, Dragon. Your own society in on the verge of sliding down the slippery slope of the mountain, too. And it won't take a century for the final tumble. As you have so wisely reminded us both, your economic growth is moving so rapidly that time frames have been compressed into months, instead of decades.

But, instead of us wringing our claws, and commiserating about the problem, how about some specifics? You're a bird of action, with sharp vision. Without offering a laundry list of vague "to dos," what must we do to survive and thrive?

Well, first of all, have your parents in the East had "the talk" with your children?

*(raising its eyebrows)* You mean the awkward one to explain where babies come from, called "the birds and the bees"?

*(shaking its head vigorously)* No, not that one, Dragon. The one parents rarely share with their children, that "money doesn't grow on trees!" Money is the least discussed subject in Western households. It seems that parents don't want their kids to know how much they are struggling to go from paycheck to paycheck.

這真的是問題，我們也一樣。我們給孩子金錢，而不是時間，但孩子在存錢和用錢上，還是搞不懂怎麼拿捏和選擇。他們把父母親看成大撲滿，裡面的現金取之不竭。

龍兄，我的想法可能太過簡單，但我們須要教導下一代什麼是「價值」。最容易的方法，就是從錢的價值開始。這樣可以馬上抓住他們的注意力，因為他們已經習慣於立即享受。

老兄，這不簡單。您也知道，我們的家庭比較小，所以有溺愛孩子的傾向。我們的子女的要求，有點兒像小皇帝和小皇后。

我們硬是擺脫不了要子女愛我們的老觀念，所以覺得有義務把我們以前沒有的給他們。可是，不讓他們學習自主和自律，其實是在剪去幼鵰的翅膀，使他們不能也不想離巢獨立。

直到不久前，我們的孩子都還聽我們的意見，非常服從，且願意用犧牲和努力換取成果。

You've got a real problem and so do we. We give children money instead of our time, yet the children have no concept about trade-offs and choices when it comes to saving and spending. They view parents as giant piggy banks with an endless supply of cash.

It may sound like an over-simplification, Dragon, but we need to teach the next generation about "values." And the easiest way to do that is to start with the value of money. That will get their immediate attention, since they are becoming used to immediate gratification.

That won't be easy, my friend. As you know, we have smaller families than you, and there is a tendency to over-indulge them. Our sons and daughters can have expectations like little emperors and empresses.

We're stuck in the rut of wanting our children to love us so much, that we feel obliged to give them everything we never had. But not letting them learn about self-determination and self-discipline, we're clipping the wings of our Eaglets so they can't or don't want to leave the nest on their own.

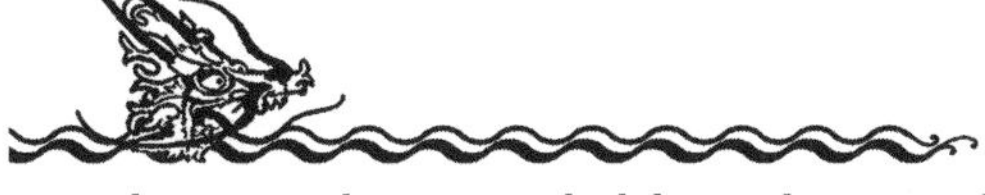

Until recently our children listened to our advice and were very obedient and willing to sacrifice and work for their rewards.

有件事可能會讓您感到驚訝。西方青少年每星期有超過一百美元的零用錢。我們給他們的，是「奪與利」，而非「根與翼」。

*（往後靠，嘆氣）*這些錢，比我們許多勞工每星期用來養家的錢還多。既然伸手就有，何必努力呢？

我們不能再當孩子的「金牛」或「搖錢樹」了。我們該做的是好榜樣和好老師。

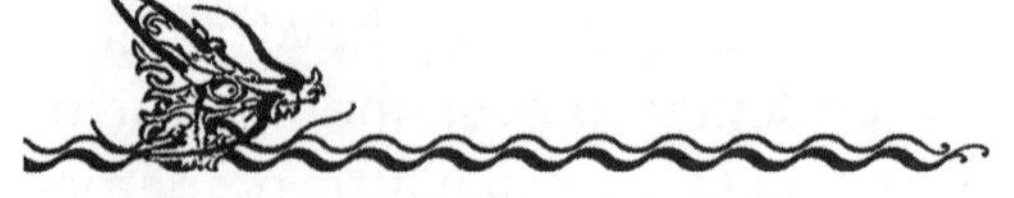

您建議我們怎麼辦？有哪些是你們沒做，但我們該做的？

有一個，你們千萬不要答應給孩子「信用卡」。對你們來說，這不會太難，因為你們向來會把收入的三成以上存起來以備不時之需。我們西方呢，現在是花的比賺的多，所以儲蓄率是負的。

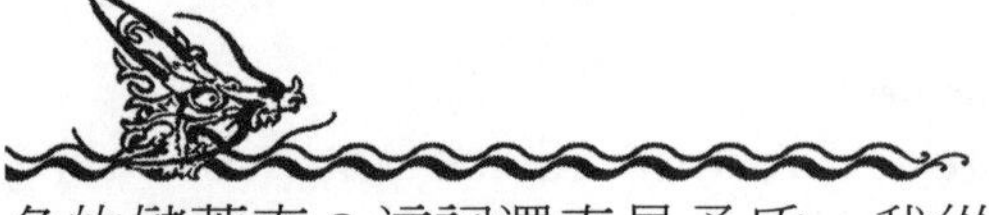

負的儲蓄率？這詞還真是矛盾，我從來沒聽過！

It may shock you to learn that the average teenagers in the West receive over $100 per week to spend however they want. We are offering them "loot and things" instead of "roots and wings."

*(leaning back on its haunches, with a sigh)* Why, that's more money per week than many of our workers earn each month to feed the entire family. Why put forth effort, when it's doled out?

We've got to put a halt to being "cash cows" and "money trees" for our kids, and become worthy role models and mentors.

So what are you suggesting we both can do? And what can we do that you aren't doing?

Well, for one thing, you must resist giving in to credit cards for your children. That shouldn't be too difficult since you have a history of saving over 30 percent of your income for the future. We, on the other hand, currently spend more than we make, and have a negative savings rate in the West.

A minus savings rate? That's an oxymoron completely foreign to me!

對我們來說，這種心態叫「現在買，但絕不付錢」。我們巧妙地把信用卡債移轉到房貸上。這樣一來，全家度假時花的錢，就可以用卅年攤還，最後孩子繼承的，是一間毫無價值的房子。

我們東方社會沈迷的是現金，而不是靠信用卡借錢。我們能存活數十個世紀，一直都是因為我們省吃儉用，為長遠的目標犧牲眼前的享受。

可是，強迫你們建立信用卡文化的壓力，幾乎會讓你們難以承受。像我們現在只關心*月付多少*，而不在意*投資可換許多少價值*。我們雙方都必須教導孩子捨棄「信用卡」，而改用「記帳卡」，這樣戶頭裡有多少，就只能花多少。

這招目前有用嗎？

這就像到牙醫那兒做根管治療但不打麻藥一樣，是條千辛萬苦的路。孩子講手機和發簡訊的費用通常都很高，也認為應該由父母負擔。我們現在還有夏令營教孩子基本的理財、規劃和穩重的投資技巧。

您是說你們已經開始把孩子成批送去學理財？

We call it the "buy now, pay never" mentality. It takes real ingenuity to transfer credit card debt over to the mortgage on our homes. In this way, we can pay for a family vacation for the next thirty years and then let our children inherit the home, which has no equity.

We in the East revel in being a cash society, rather than a credit card debt society. Our survival throughout the centuries has been based on being thrifty and sacrificing immediate pleasure for long-term goals.

But the pressure will be almost insurmountable for you to become a credit card culture, like us, more interested in the *monthly payment* than in the *investment versus value*. We both must teach our children to replace credit cards with debit cards,where they can only spend what is in their own bank accounts.

Is this working for you?

It's like having a root canal at the dentist—without anesthesia. It's an uphill battle. Our children often have large mobile phone and text messaging bills that they expect their parents to pay. There are now summer camps teaching our kids basic skills in money management, budgeting, and prudent investing.

So you are beginning to ship them off to "money schools"?

可以這麼說，但一切都要從家裡開始。孩子應該視年齡和家庭所得領零用錢。我認為每月或每星期給零用錢，是學習健全理財觀念的基本步驟。

所以若他們把房間整理乾淨，或者學校功課好，你們就會給錢？

我們是經過辛苦地邊試邊學，才發現男孩和女孩應該拿同額且定額的零用錢，目的在於讓他們學習管理個人的需求和慾求，而不在於收買或給錢來鼓勵學習或獎勵個人儀容。

可是，老師以前不是說做得越多越好，報酬就越多？

沒錯，但做家事、保持房間整潔和用功讀書，應該是一種自我驅策，而不是賄賂。父母親也沒因為煮飯、打掃和處理個人事務而拿錢。我認為，孩子為全家的福利做做家事，也不該拿錢。

您同意付出額外努力，就該有額外獎勵嗎？去外面打工，也能學習到額外努力會有回報。

Sort of, but it all begins in the home. Children should be given allowances, appropriate to their ages and the family income. I believe these monthly or weekly cash allowances are fundamental steps toward learning healthy money management.

So do you pay them for keeping their rooms and things tidy, or for doing well in their studies at school?

We have learned the hard way, through trial and error, that male and female children should receive an equal, set amount of money to manage for personal needs and wants, not as bribes or incentives for being motivated to learn or personal grooming.

But aren't we taught if we do more and better work, we'll get more pay raises?

Yes, but doing chores, keeping your room tidy and studying should be an inner drive, not a payoff. Mothers and fathers are not paid for cooking, cleaning and managing their personal affairs at home. So the children should not, in my opinion, be given money for chores that they should do as contributors to the family well being.

But you do agree that doing extra work beyond regular chores could result in an extra bonus? And having a job outside the home also teaches that extra effort is rewarded.

當然啦。孩子的功課或課外活動表現好時，應該特地安排出遊或合適的慶祝活動，好強化他們的努力。研究顯示，孩子的學習動力，若是來自內在或既有的動機，如靠自己追求卓越或成就，他們的專業貢獻會優於看錢做事者。熱愛你所做，遠強過為外在獎勵而做。

在這個重物質和地位的世界裡，我們該如何培養不屈不撓且眼光長遠的下一代？

這方面，到目前為止，你們的表現比我們好，但不要以為文化傳統可以抵擋潮流。我們終於開始教孩子把零用錢分成四個部分。我就以四個裝茶葉或香料用的玉瓶子做譬喻：第一瓶標示著**花用**；第二個**儲蓄**；第三個**分享**；第四個**未來**。

恕我冒昧，您不覺得用玉瓶子有點落伍嗎？現在絕大部分的幼龍都會用電腦，連小的都有手機和掌上型設備。

瓶子或罐子絕對適用於介於三到六、七歲的小孩身上。過了這個年紀後，就應該開存款與支票帳戶。「記帳卡」或「現金卡」會視存款而限定提款額度，也不能用來借錢，也是值得考慮的工具。我國

No question. And doing well in school or extra-curricular events should warrant a special outing or appropriate ceremony to reinforce the effort. Our research has shown that children who are motivated to learn via internal or intrinsic motivations such as a desire for excellence or achievement by independent action, do much better in their professional contributions than those who are driven by money. Loving what you do is more powerful than the love for external rewards.

In this era of materialism, and status, how can we both develop more perseverance, resilience and long-term thinking in our children?

Well, so far, you're doing a better job than we are in that regard, but don't think your cultural traditions can stem the tide. We finally are trying to teach our young children to put their allowances in four categories. Using the analogy of four jade jars that you may have used for storing different kinds of tea or spices, label the first jar SPEND; the second jar SAVE; the third jar SHARE; and the fourth jar FUTURE.

Don't you think using jars is a bit antiquated, if I do say so myself? Even our young Dragons are becoming computer literate rapidly, and even the little ones have mobile phones and hand-held devices.

Jars or canisters are certainly appropriate for children from about 3 to 6 or 7 years of age. After that, checking and savings accounts should be opened. And consider debit cards or cash cards that they can use to withdraw funds depending on their

最嚴重的社會問題之一，就是信用卡債。

既然如此，不管是瓶子還是戶頭，要怎麼教孩子管理這四類零用錢？

假設有個五歲的孩子每星期有五塊美金的零用錢。換算成你們的幣值是多少我不知道，您自己算吧！這樣每個月就有廿元。

鵰兄，別鬧了…五歲拿這些錢太多了吧！

這只夠每星期吃個巨無霸漢堡和一份薯條，不能吃甜點也不能看電影。我看不出多久，所有的五歲孩子都會覺得每星期至少要有廿元。

*（發牢騷）*這樣東西方的孩子看起來全會像相撲選手。

balances, with no borrowing power. Credit card debt is one of the biggest problems in our society.

All right then, whether its jars or bank accounts, how do you demonstrate the four categories of managing allowances for children?

Let's say your five-year-old receives an allowance of $5 per week. I don't know how many *yuan* that is, but you can do the math. That amounts to $20 per month.

Come on, Eagle...that sounds overly generous for a five-year-old!

That's only one Big Mac and an order of fries per week, with no dessert and no movies. It won't be long until all of our five-year-olds expect at least $20 per week.

*(grumbling)* And all of our children East and West will begin to look like Sumo wrestlers.

*（輕笑）*我要說的不多，讓我說完。第一個標著**花用**的瓶子，裡面要放三成，也就是六塊錢，好用在這個月想買的東西上。第二個瓶子裡，孩子要**儲蓄**五成，也就是十塊錢，好用在今年某個特別的東西或場合上。第三個瓶子，裡頭要放一成，也就是二塊錢，好與別人**分享**，像是給祖父母買禮物，或者捐給慈善機構。第四個罐子要放一成，也就是二塊錢，好為**未來**做準備。這筆錢絕不能動用，是未來經濟保障的第一步。

鵰兄，這個觀念我喜歡。東西方的父母都絕對需要一些明確的指導。我也希望看到幼龍把超過一成的零用錢留給未來。可是，我知道您為什麼向西方提出這樣的建議。對負的儲蓄率來說，一成算是巨幅的進步了！

我知道在您面前談先苦後甘是班門弄斧。幾個世紀以來東方都展現了這個特質。我只是希望你們能從我們身上學到教訓，而我們也能從你們過往興衰的教訓中學習。

通過這樣的討論，我們或許會意識到答案和解藥原來就在問題裡。

*(chuckling)* Let me finish my little speech. In jar one, the child puts 30%, or $6, to SPEND on whatever he or she wants this month. In jar two, the child puts 50%, or $10, to SAVE for some special item or event later in the year. In jar three, the child puts 10%, or $2, to SHARE, for a gift for someone else, like a grandparent or a worthy charity. In jar four, the child puts the final 10%, or $2, for the FUTURE. The money that accumulates in that jar is never spent and becomes the first step toward future financial security.

I like the concept, Eagle. Heaven knows parents need some specific guidelines in both of our cultures. I would like to see our Dragon children put more than 10% of their allowances aside for the FUTURE. But I understand why you are suggesting that for the West. Ten percent is a huge, positive leap from a negative savings rate!

I realize I am preaching to the choir when I say anything to you about delayed gratification. The East has demonstrated this quality for centuries. I just hope you learn from our mistakes, and that we can learn from all that you have gleaned from your past peaks and valleys.

By discussing these issues, perhaps we will find answers and solutions residing within the problems themselves.

當然，我想您也知道西方的家庭正面臨危機。許多研究顯示，西方的婚姻品質在婚後四年內開始變質，然後會持續十年左右，接著繼續惡化。西方婚姻多視孩子為一大壓力來源，東方在這方面或許看法不同。很遺憾的，離婚率不斷在攀升

鵬兄，這兒也不例外，但我得指出許多年前，婚姻是父母安排的；未來的媳婦沒什麼決定權。以前沒什麼離婚，做妻子想要求離婚也無法可循。可是，做丈夫想休妻則至少有七個理由可以挑。（或許還可以更多，但我只想得到七個。）

*（開始微笑，然後變嚴肅，不想得罪龍）*七個？這根本不公平，不是嗎？

鵬兄，這跟公不公平沒關係。我們談的是歷史事實。今天雖然不這樣了，但讓丈夫可以像鵬般遠走高飛的七個理由如下：一、不視舅姑；二、口舌；三、淫佚；四、盜竊；五、惡疾；六、嫉妒；七、無子（最糟）。這些當然不公平，但過去就是這樣。

龍族一直到一九二零及三零年代，才開始擺脫此一傳統，不靠父母親的安排而自由戀愛。這個改變確實很激進。新的政治理念，再加上投入感情這個曠古未聞的觀念，使舊傳統慢慢開始瓦解。

Certainly, I think you already know that families in the West are in crisis. Much of the research tells us the quality of marriages in the West begins to decline within the first four years after the ceremony. It then stays at that level for the next ten years or so, and then drops again. Unlike the East, perhaps, Western marriages, in many cases, regard the presence of children as a great stress on the marriage. Sadly, the rate of divorce continues to rise.

It's happening here too, Eagle, but I must say that many years ago marriages were arranged by parents; and wives-to-be had very little say-so in the matter. In days past, divorce was rare and no divorce proceeding could ever be initiated by the wife. However, the husband had at least seven reasons for leaving a marriage. (There may be more ways, but I can only think of seven.)

*(starting to smile, then becoming serious, not wanting to offend Dragon)* Seven? That hardly seems fair, does it?

Eagle, we're not talking about what's fair or unfair. We're talking about the facts of history. Although this isn't the case today, those seven ways for a husband to *fly the coop,* as an Eagle might put it, were: 1. if the wife refused to obey her husband or his parents; 2. if she talked too much; 3. if she were morally loose; 4. if she were caught stealing; 5. if she had a transmittable disease; 6. if she were jealous; or 7. if, perish the thought, she could not bear a child. No, it definitely wasn't fair, but that's the way it was.

It was only in the late 1920s and '30s that our Dragons began to break free from tradition to select their own mates without their union being arranged by their parents. That was a radical move indeed. Slowly, the old order began to collapse due to new political attitudes and, a first for us—*emotional commitments.*

目前的狀況呢？東方的家庭還是像以前一樣緊密嗎？離婚率呢?

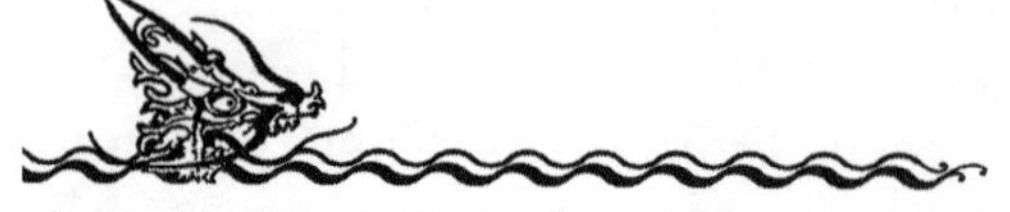

我認為今天的家庭甚至比以前還緊密，但毫無疑問的，寬鬆的婚姻法導致了離婚率上升。讓我這條老龍著實嚇一跳的，是女性現在會去「婚友社」找對象。她們大多被拋棄，因為前夫有外遇，且對象比她們年輕了十到十五歲。

這種情況我無法接受，但在東方，甚至我這老龍的話，也不是每個人都願意聽的。我最厭惡的，是新的離婚法似乎對丈夫有利。性別平等這方面，我們要走的路還很遠。

在西方，離婚通常交由律師或法官處理，有時則找調解人。最後，雙方會簽署一份文件，內容清楚描述離婚條件、分居時間、贍養費、財產分配及孩子的監護權。整個過程不一定平順，但我們鵰是這麼處理的。

這兒不太一樣，鵰兄。我們在東方可以付個五十元，等兩個星期，然後就突然結婚，大家依據傳統高興地喝喜酒，最後急忙說個再見就結束了。這兒的離婚率，相對來說比西方國家低，但在不斷上升中。

不知道您記不記得，我說過我們在街上遇見朋友時，打招呼的方式是：「吃過了嗎？」各大城市裡現在流傳著一個笑話。在街上碰到朋友時，可能會聽到新的問候方法：*「離了嗎？」*

So how is it in the East today? Is the family as solid as it was in the past? And what about divorce?

I believe the family is even more solid than in the past, although there's no question that tolerant marriage laws are contributing to a rising of our divorce rate. One thing that astounds this old Dragon is that women are now turning to "dating agencies" to find new husbands. Many of these are women who've been left alone after their husbands abandon them for women 10–15 years younger.

Personally, I don't like it at all. But even here in the East not everyone is willing to listen to an old Dragon. What I dislike most is that the new divorce laws seem to favor the husband. We need to do much more about gender equality!

In the West, divorce cases are usually handled by lawyers, judges and occasionally by mediators. In the end, there's a legal document with two signatures that clearly describes the terms of the divorce, established length of separation, alimony, if any, division of the property, and custody of the children. It may not be a pleasant process, but, this is how Eagles deal with it.

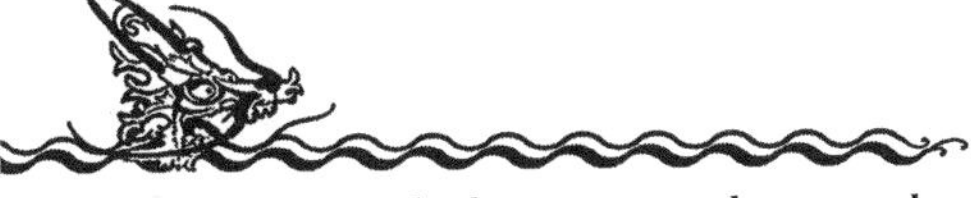

Not so as much here, Eagle. In the East Dragons can pay something like 50 *yuan*. After waiting for two weeks, they suddenly see a marriage that began with a long-established festive feast end with a hasty good bye. The divorce rate here is still relatively low compared to those in Western nations. But it's increasing steadily.

Do you remember how I told you we often ask, "Have you eaten?" when we meet people on the street—our form of "hello"? Well there's now a joke circulating in our major cities. Often when people meet a friend on the street, you're just as apt to hear a new question: *Li le ma?—Have you divorced?*

不太好笑吧，龍兄？

鵰兄，一點兒都不好笑！經濟成長帶動著社會的變革，甚至政府對個人生活的干預也很少了，而許多朋友認為社會最大的變革之一，就是離婚這麼容易。個人享有了前所未見的自由。可是，我要問我們究竟是否在用新的自主權做該做的事。我擔心這種趨勢，到最後會影響我們做的每一件事。以前啊，東方的年輕人不必提醒，就會照顧父母或祖父母。今天呢，電視廣告的結尾居然是…*記得關心父母親*。這個趨勢讓我擔心：孩子越來越不敬老。

可是，一旦中了愛神的箭，不管你是鵰還是龍，就沒藥救了。我知道幾年前東方最紅的書之一，是「*麥迪遜之橋*」，故事描述一位寂寞的中年婦女，因為外遇才得到期盼已久的浪漫。我也知道許多東方女性，晚上會跟朋友圍坐討論書中描述的浪漫情節，可不可能在婚姻中發生。

鵰兄，您應該看得出我這齜牙咧嘴的，跟浪漫小說不太搭調。可是，我瞭解這類書對幼龍為什麼有吸引力。這樣吧，鵰兄，我請教一個問題。家庭失去靈魂的話，文化、社會與人民還能存續多久？經濟成長了，「科技小玩意兒」多了，家庭卻沒了該怎麼辦？這樣值得嗎？

Not very funny, is it, Dragon?

No Eagle, it's not funny at all! In a land where our economic growth is changing the social landscape—and where there is even less official interference in individual lives—many see the ease of divorce as one of the most dramatic changes in our society. We have more personal freedom than ever. But I question if we are using our new found self-determination to do the right thing. Ultimately, I'm afraid this trend will affect everything we do. In the past, no young person in the East would need to be reminded to take care of his or her parents or grandparents. Today, we're watching television ads ending with words such as...*Don't forget your parents.* This is a trend that troubles me: Children are losing respect for their elders.

But once the love bug bites Eagles or Dragons, there's no medicine anywhere to heal the patient? In fact, I understand that one of the most popular books in the East some years ago was *The Bridges of Madison County*, the story of a midlife affair that brings long awaited romance to a lonely woman's life. I understand many Eastern women would spend evenings sitting around with friends, discussing whether the romance described in the book is possible in a marriage.

Well, Eagle, I'm a bit long in the fangs to read romantic novels, if you know what I mean. But I do see the attraction such books hold for our young Dragons. So, Eagle, let me ask you this: How long can a culture, a society, and a people survive and thrive if the family unit loses its soul? So what if we gain economically and have more "gadgets" and lose our families? What is the value in that?

我覺得我今天說話有些太負面了。年輕男女都比較晚婚生子。女性珍惜事業，男性必須負擔更多家事及養育子女的責任。這樣的好處，是婚姻的關係越來越平等，不再只是男主外女主內。職場也越來越平等。女性終於得到老早就該擁有的機會，能夠領導公司、機構和政府。薪資上的平等，希望也能趕快實現。

有些都市裡的年輕專業人士，其中包含女性，就像在西方一樣選擇晚婚，有些夫妻則喜歡當領雙薪不生孩子的「頂客族」。男性結婚的平均年齡是28歲，女性是27歲。

正如您剛才所說，我們今天喝茶交流，變得有點兒像在「相互憐憫」。可是，家庭生活大幅度改變，並不一定不好。個人的選擇與自由越來越受重視，性別越來越平等，甚至跟過去的大家庭比起來，親子關係也越來越親密。

媳婦在家庭的地位也已經提升，因為她通常要負責照顧長輩。雖然今天的家庭人數比較少，「家庭事業」的觀念仍舊盛行。「財星前五百大公司」裡面，有三分之一來自我國的家庭企業，這點您知道嗎？

不知道，但我怎麼一點也不驚訝？貴國真的是把「全家一起來」的口號發揮到極致！雖然我們的風俗不同，語言和方言也不同，但我

I fear I've been a bit too gloomy in today's exchange. Young men and women are waiting longer to marry and have children in our society. Women value their careers and husbands are expected to help more with household chores and raising children. The good news is that marriages have become more of an equal partnership, rather than the male being the earner and the female the sole caretaker of the home. This is leading to more parity in professional life as well, with women finally receiving long overdue and well-deserved opportunities to lead companies, institutions and governments. Hopefully, equality in pay will soon follow.

As in the West, some of our urban, young professionals, including women, are choosing to remain single, while some couples prefer to be "dinks," or double-income-no-kids. The average age of marriage in our land is 28 for men and 27 for women.

And, as you pointed out, we almost turned today's tea drinking conversation into a mutual "pity party." Just because family life is changing dramatically, that doesn't necessarily mean it is in decline. There is more emphasis on personal choice and freedom, more equality in the sexes and even a stronger bond between parents and children than under the collective security of the previous era.

The daughter-in-law has gained more status in our families, since she usually is in charge of care for the elder members. And although we have much smaller family units today, the concept of "family businesses" continues to flourish. Were you aware that our family businesses account for one-third of the names on your "Fortune 500" list of the world's biggest companies?

No, but why am I not surprised? Your country certainly epitomizes the banner of "All in the Family!" Although many of our customs are different and we speak different languages and

們對成功的願景大體一致。龍兄，關鍵在於我們不斷地溝通、聆聽和交流，也就是正如您說過的，咱們*多喝茶聊聊。*

鵰兄，有時您的智慧似乎超越年齡。現在是該我向您學習的時候了。我曾讀過其它雕寫的書。最近有篇題為貧窮的文章，吸引了我的注意。我之所以注意，是因為我想知道我們是否都真如預期般富裕。

讀過那篇文章後，我就不確定了。鵰兄，我今天想留幾句話給您。雖然是西方的觀念，但還是與您來自東方的龍族新朋友們息息相關。以下就是我最近讀的那篇文章…

貧窮

- 貧窮就是未經考驗的潛能，源自於自我設限。
- 貧窮就是衣服明明很多，但覺得「沒一件能穿」。
- 貧窮就是有三個學位，但工作上卻沒有成就感。
- 貧窮就是工作一個接著一個，客戶一個接著一個，「買賣」一個接著一個，且永遠沒法兒停下來享受外面世界的美麗。
- 貧窮就是非常缺乏安全感，覺得必須順從他人才會被接受。
- 貧窮就是對周遭的世界從不好奇，從不想探索它或認識其中的人。
- 貧窮可以是精神上的，也可以是身體上的。

dialects, we continue to hold many of the same visions for success. The key, Dragon, is for us to keep talking...to keep listening...and to keep communicating and, as you say, *keep drinking lots of tea together.*

Eagle, sometimes you seem wise beyond your years. Now it's I who needs to spend more time listening to you. Meanwhile, I have been reading what your other Eagles have been writing. One short essay titled "Poverty" caught my attention recently. I was drawn to this because I wonder if we both are really becoming as rich as we think we are.

After reading this, I'm no longer sure. Eagle, I'd like to leave these thoughts with you today—ideas that come from the West, but that are just as pertinent to your new Dragon colleagues in the East. Here's what I read recently...

POVERTY

- Poverty is untested potential, resulting from self-imposed limitations.
- Poverty is having so many clothes, you "haven't a thing to wear."
- Poverty is having three academic degrees and feeling unfulfilled in your job.
- Poverty is going day-to-day from one job to the next, one building to the next, one "deal" to the next and never stopping to enjoy the beauty in the world outside.
- Poverty is being so insecure that you feel you must be someone else to be accepted.
- Poverty is never being curious about the world around you and never wanting to explore it or the people in it.
- Poverty is as much of the soul as it is the body.

就這樣，龍與鵬又結束了一天的精彩交流。一整天努力地相互瞭解…而這一天，雙方極力想瞭解*家庭*一詞對東西方的意義。就在鵬沒入雲中的同時，龍仍在思考東方究竟是貧是富。目前還無法下任何定論。或許下一次見面，鵬能提供更現代的實際經驗。此外，龍希望鵬能接受他這個新老朋友的忠告。

And so passed another day of spirited dialog between the Eagle and the Dragon. Another long day of working toward mutual understanding. . .and on this day, desiring to comprehend what *family* means to the East and to the West. As the Eagle disappeared into the clouds, the Dragon continued to ponder where the East was on the rich/poor scale. Any final decisions on this would have to wait. Perhaps the Eagle would be forthcoming with yet more contemporary, learn-from-experience insights the next time they met. And, the Dragon hoped the Eagle would heed some of the admonitions of his new but elder friend.

# 摘要

第四回

# Summary

CHAPTER 4

## 家庭第一

## Family First

# 龍親口告訴我們…
# Straight from the Dragon's mouth...

☯ 現代東方社會的互動，較著重愛情與金錢，而不只是單純的敬老而已。約會與戀愛是流行，三代同堂則越來越過時。如此社會轉變，影響的是整個社會，其中包含個人與商業。

☯ 我們**為家人在家中與家人共事**。我們選擇不與外人分享此一信任感。然而，這種心態有好有壞。同時，鵰族絕對不能假設自己能夠穿透這個年深日久的保護層。

☯ In the East today, our social dynamic is more about love and money than simply respecting our elders. Dating and falling love are in vogue; living under the same roof with parents and grandparents is becoming passé. This societal shift has ramifications for our entire society—personal and business.

☯ We work ***with*** our family, ***within*** the family and ***for*** the family. We do not choose to share our trust with outsiders. This position, however, presents both a strength and a weakness. Meanwhile, you Eagles must never assume that you will penetrate our long-established shell of protection.

## 鵰的看法則是…
# From the Eagle's point of view...

✷ 鵰多年來遵循自立的信念。數以百萬計的龍，現在不得不正視這個議題。不瞭解這個社會轉變，就不算瞭解現代東方。

✷ 西方婚姻常視孩子為夫妻關係的壓力來源。東方一向卻不是如此。然而，一胎化政策逐漸成熟後，無數的龍正在創造自己的「空巢期症候群」。部分家庭壓力可能因此消失；但寂寞的現象也非常普遍。

✷ Eagles have lived with the idea of personal independence for many years. Millions of Dragons are just now being compelled to deal with this issue. Not to be aware of this societal shift is not to understand today's East.

✷ Western marriages often regard the presence of children as a stress on relationships. Historically, this was never true of the East. However, with the maturing of the one-child policy, millions of Dragons are creating their own "empty nest syndromes." This may remove some familial stress; it also is producing loneliness on a grand scale.

# 龍親口告訴我們…
# Straight from the Dragon's mouth...

☯ 東方到處可見以***別忘孝順父母***為結尾的電視廣告。如此隨處不在的提醒，顯示這個一度受尊崇的家庭傳統，已在式微中。鵰必須瞭解這個社會發展趨勢。

☯ 從貧窮心態迅速轉變為**致富**心態，已對家庭造成傷害。對財富的追求，已使無數的龍遠遠落後，那些守著「老家」的老龍數目，更已不斷創下新高。社會各階層一股腦追求「金錢文化」，可能使東方面對的挑戰加劇，出現意料之外的結果。

☯ The East is now blanketed with television ads ending with words such as...***Don't forget your parents.*** This ever-present reminder is indicative of where our once-honored family tradition is heading. Eagles must be aware of these shifts in our society.

☯ To move so quickly from a poverty state of mind to a ***get rich*** mentality is taking its toll on the family. The pursuit of wealth is leaving millions of our Dragons in the dust—particularly the elderly who inhabit our "old Dragons" homes in greater numbers than ever. At all levels, our head-long pursuit of a "money culture" could further challenge the East and give us results we hadn't counted on.

## 鵰的看法則是…

# *From the Eagle's point of view...*

✶ 若您是浪漫小說的作家，東方可能有無數的龍在期待您的新作。若*麥迪遜之橋*能擠進暢銷書排行榜，之後以此禁忌為題的書應該也能。

✶ 許多鵰認為，龍與外人做生意時，以管制和保護為手段，促進了東方商業的繁榮。除非東方與鵰做生意時能更透明、信任且開放，否則不可能營造雙贏局面。

✶ If you are a writer of romantic novels, the East may be where millions of Dragons are awaiting your next creative endeavor. If *Bridges of Madison County* can make the best seller list in the East, so will subsequent books that treat this once taboo subject.

✶ Many Eagles see an Eastern business environment that thrives on keeping control and maintaining an advantage when it comes to engaging in business relationships outside the Dragon's family. Unless the East becomes more transparent, trusting and open in business relationships with Eagles, there will never be a win-win situation.

# 龍親口告訴我們…
# Straight from the Dragon's mouth...

☯ 東方對貧窮的瞭解，史上少有民族能相比擬。然而，當我讀了西方的…***貧窮就是工作一個接著一個，客戶一個接著一個，「買賣」一個接著一個，且永遠沒法兒停下來享受外面世界的美麗***…之後，不禁思考我們究竟多「富裕」。我們必須關心金錢與權勢以外的問題。

☯ 我們應在孩子身上多花時間，少花錢。

☯ The East has known poverty as few nations in history. However, when I read the Western words...***Poverty is going day-to-day from one job to the next, one building to the next, one "deal" to the next and never stopping to enjoy the beauty in the world outside,*** I'm forced to wonder how "rich" we really are. We need to attend to issues other than money and power.

☯ We should spend more time with our children and less money on them.

## 鵰的看法則是…

## *From the Eagle's point of view...*

✯ 鵰並非十全十美。我們有許多令人喜愛的特質，但我們像世界各地的龍與鵰一樣，也會欺騙與操弄。好消息是我們設計了許多機制，以保護可能因他人貪婪而可能受害者。龍族也必須如此，否則雙方無法建立雙贏關係。

✯ 我們必須給孩子「根與翼」，而非「奪與利」。親身給予孩子支持，是愛的最佳表現。

✯ Eagles are not perfect. We have many attributes to be admired, but we also deceive and manipulate—like Dragons and Eagles everywhere. The good news is that we are now putting into place safeguards to protect potential victims of another's greed. Dragons must do the same if we're to enjoy a win-win relationship.

✯ We need to give our kids "roots and wings" instead of "loot and things." The best gift of love is being there for them in person.

第五回

CHAPTER 5

# 文化挑戰

# Cultural Challenges

**龍**與鵬的話匣子一旦開了，就很難再關上。好幾個月前，鵬第一次急速掠過地面上的巨大岩縫，只想一窺其中的龐然巨物。然而，龍現在只要聽見鵬拍動雙翼的聲音，就會開始沏茶，為另一回合發人省思的對話做好準備。不管怎麼看，龍與鵬似乎是對剛結識的「歡喜冤家」，但他們可不這麼認為。他們已經成為好朋友。更適切的說法，應該是好同事。

龍與鵬第一次見面時，經常相互猜疑：***鵬說的話，不知道是不是都能信…龍這麼老，怎麼可能跟得上國家的最新發展…鵬這麼年輕，又心浮氣躁。好歹我也該試試看，至少假裝我在聽這個長翅膀的朋友說話。要龍改大概很難，但若我也過過五千多個生日，應該也會這樣吧。***

可是，過了這麼多個月以後，相互猜疑已經慢慢轉變為相互信任與尊重。雙方都越來越願意聽對方的觀點。不論是龍穴還是鵬巢，都還有這麼多值得學習之處。商業關係仍然是熱門的話題。相對的世界觀，一向值得花幾個小時深入討論…除此之外，還有許多可以談。*過去*，他們的差異的確很大，但他們的交情越深，就越覺得差異其實可能沒這麼大。

這讓鵬想起莎士比亞的戲 — *威尼斯商人*，其中猶太人夏洛克的種族背景遭到批評，而他的回應是：「*你刺我，難道我不流血嗎？你搔我，難道我不笑嗎？你毒我，難道我不死嗎？你錯怪我，難道我不報仇嗎？既然別的事我們跟你們一樣，那這些我們還是跟你們一樣。*」

儘管龍與鵬知道雙方沒這麼不同，但也知道一些主要的文化差異仍須面對。讓我們繼續聽聽我們的兩位朋友這次喝茶會聊什麼。

龍兄，您覺得我們談到目前為止，有沒有任何實用價值，還是太過抽象？我知道我們有時茶一沏就是好幾個小時，話一談就談到凌

Once Dragon and Eagle got to talking, it was difficult for them to stop. It had now been several months since Eagle had first swooped over the great fissure in the earth, wondering about the awesome creature that lay below. However, now when Dragon would hear the telltale flapping of Eagle's wings, it would put on a pot of tea and make ready for another round of thought-provoking conversation. From all appearances it would seem that Dragon and Eagle were the latest manifestation of the "odd couple." But the two of them didn't see it that way. They had now become good friends. Colleagues, in fact.

When Dragon and Eagle first met each other, there were many suspicious moments between them: *I don't know if I can really believe everything Eagle has to say*... ***Dragon is really old, and I wonder how it can possibly be up to date on what's happening in its country***... *Eagle is so young and excitable. But I suppose I can give it a chance and at least pretend I'm learning something from my winged friend*... ***Dragon seems to be set in its ways. But I guess that's natural when you've had more than 5,000 birthdays.***

However, these many months later, the mutual suspicion had slowly turned into mutual trust and respect. Both were increasingly opening their ears to listen to the other's point of view. There was still so much to learn about life in both Dragon- and Eagleland. Business relationships remained a hot topic. The subject of opposing world views was always worth a few hours of discussion...all this and so much more. To be sure, there were great differences between them. However, the more they got to know each other, the greater the feeling that they might not be that different after all.

This reminded Eagle of William Shakespeare's play *Merchant of Venice*, where Shylock, a Jew, was responding to criticisms regarding his ethnicity. Shylock said, *If you prick us, do we not bleed? If you tickle us, do we not laugh? If you poison us, do we not die? And if you wrong us, shall we not revenge? If we are like you in the rest, we will resemble you in that.*

But alike as they were, Eagle and Dragon still knew they needed to deal with several major cultural differences. And so we listen in on our two friends as they engage in yet another tea party discussion.

Dragon, do you think what we've been talking about has had enough practical application, or have we been overly philosophical? I know sometimes we keep the tea kettle on for hours as we talk into the wee hours of the morning—but to what advan-

晨，但這對其他的的龍與鵰來說，究竟有什麼幫助嗎？

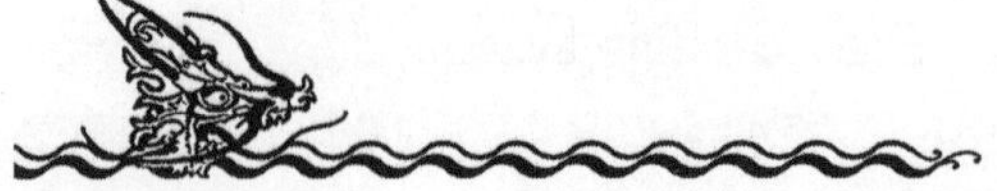

這個嘛，鵰兄，我覺得我們算是兩者兼顧了。*再來杯茶嗎？*我認為我們其實為互信立下了重要的基礎，讓龍與鵰們在學習、經商及旅遊時，能兼顧雙方文化上的不同。可是，為確保我們之間溝通順暢，咱們現在談談明顯的文化差異怎麼樣？

*（興奮地拍動翅膀）*好啊。龍兄，我們先從自我的概念談起，行嗎？我真的認為這個方面有得談了。您不介意的話，我可以起個頭嗎？

請便，鵰兄。我想這問題想了五千多年，大概總有一天會知道真正的「我」究竟是誰吧。畢竟，我可是集了九條不同的龍於一身！

龍兄，您還真幽默啊。我是這麼看的。我們在西方比較重視自立。我們不介意自我推銷，為了把生意做好時尤其如此。不瞞您說，有些朋友還以此為題開班授課。有了這種自立的態度，我們似乎比較重視如何不受外力的限制。龍兄，龍族對「自我」的概念似乎有所不同，對不對？

tage of other Dragons and Eagles?

Well, Eagle, my sense is that we've done a bit of both. *Would you like another cup of tea?* I actually think we've laid important groundwork for mutual understanding that our students, business Eagles and Dragons, tourists and others can use to work within our varying cultures. But to be sure we're doing a good job of communication, what do you say we focus right now on our more obvious cultural differences?

*(flapping its wings excitedly)* Let's do it. Dragon, can we start with the concept of how we regard the self? I *do* think we have some major challenges here. I'll start, if that's okay.

Be my guest, Eagle. Perhaps after over 5,000 years of contemplating this subject, I'll get to know the real "me." After all, I am nine different characters all rolled into one!

Very funny, Dragon. Here's how I see it. In the West we place a higher value on self-reliance. We're comfortable with the concept of self-promotion, particularly when it comes into play as we work toward success in business. In fact, we even have seminars on this subject. And with this self-oriented behavior, we seem to place a higher value on freedom from constraints forced upon us from the outside. Am I correct, Dragon, that you and your fellow Dragons might see the idea of "self" in a different light?

沒錯，鵰兄，的確滿不同的。我們絕對比較重視合作與謙讓。我們不太喜歡…*你們怎麼說來著…自顧自的猛按喇叭*。這個傾向現在可能有些改變了，原因就在於眾鵰們對我們的影響。可是，我們的天性基本上仍是合群，服從領導指示，以社會群體為重。我看這是天性，永遠改不了。

有趣。我們雖然比較強調競爭，但我們的體制也重視個別意見。不承認我們之間有所差異是個大錯，但我們或許在這方面能相互學習。不然，你們可能會覺得鵰太傲慢自大，而我們也可能覺得龍太循規蹈矩。我想我們對友誼的看法也是這樣。

鵰兄啊，我看我們混在一起太久了…因為我下一個想談的，剛好也是友誼。我們龍族一切以家庭為中心。就算不是家人，也得是親近的老朋友才行。正是這一方面，我覺得我們的看法會非常不同。在這個由朋友與同事組成的緊密圈子裡，存在著一種深刻不變的忠誠感；說它是義務也行，使我們願意為朋友兩肋插刀。鵰兄，跟我們做生意時有一點很重要，最好不要忘記。我們不是不歡迎你們，而是我們深信一個觀念：對密友與家人越信任，對自己越有好處。

Oh yes, Eagle. Quite different, indeed. We definitely place a higher value on group cooperation and individual modesty. We do not feel good about, how do you say it?...*tooting our own horn very much*. This may be changing somewhat—largely because of the influence you and your Eagles are exerting on us. However, it's still our basic nature to fit in with the group at large, listen obediently to our leaders for direction, and cooperate with society as a whole. I guess it's part of our DNA. I don't think it will ever change.

Interesting. We may place more emphasis on competition, but we also have a system where every vote is supposed to count. Not to recognize our differences would be a mistake, but perhaps we can take a lesson or two from each other in this matter. Otherwise, Eagles may appear to you to be overly arrogant, while Dragons may seem to us to be overly compliant. I think it's the same with how we view friendships.

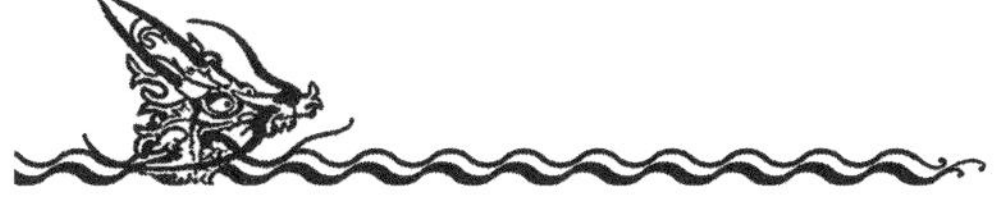

Ah Eagle, we've been together too long...because *friendship* was the next topic on my list. In Dragonland, we keep things in the family. If not in the family, then at least among close, life-long friends. Here's where I have feeling we're very different. In this close coterie of friends and colleagues, there is a deep, abiding sense of loyalty—obligation, if you like—to give each other whatever assistance might be required. It's important you note this, Eagle, when you do business with us. Don't think we don't like you. Just remember there is this deeply ingrained sense that we are best served when we trust our intimate friends and family more.

這*的確*引人深省，也很有幫助。龍兄，您又說對了。我們對友誼的看法差異之大，就跟您棲身的大岩縫一樣寬。現在輪到我試著說明鵰對友誼的看法。首先，我們通常會有許多朋友、點頭之交與同事，而且不停地換。在不同的學校或公司裡我們會認識很多人，但不見得是一輩子的朋友。

我們也把客戶當朋友，但客戶一走，「友」的部分大概也沒了。龍兄，我認為其中最大的不同處，在於我們對朋友的義務有限。對家人還比較平常，在商務上就少見了。您剛說*東方會為朋友兩肋插刀時*，我的背就起了一陣陣鵰皮疙瘩。我們大概沒這麼慷慨，但你們對友誼的看法確實不同。

這也影響了雙方對社會關係的看法。咱們龍比較重形式與階級。*鵰兄，不准笑。我知道我們倆不這麼重形式，但住在這條大裂縫附近的鄉親們，大多絕不會像我們這樣真誠以對。*龍族不介意聽命行事，這樣大家才知道自己的位置…自己的本分…有什麼法令規章，且相對上變動不大。

龍兄，難怪許多朋友和你們做生意時，覺得快瘋了。我無意冒犯，但這真的讓有些朋友氣急敗壞。我告訴您為什麼。在我們的世界裡，不拘形式是種生活方式。我們重雙贏重平等。規範與界線當然

That *is* enlightening, and helpful. Again, you're right, Dragon. This gap in our view of friendship is almost as large as the fissure in the earth your massive body occupies. Let me take a stab at how the Eagles view friendships. First of all, we tend to have a large collection of friends, acquaintances and colleagues which are constantly in a state of flux. We have friends as we progress through different learning institutions or companies—but not necessarily for a lifetime.

We have client friends. But when the client goes away, so does that "friendship" for the most part. But the key difference, as I see it Dragon, is that we have limited mutual obligations to each other. It is more common in families; rare indeed in business. When you said in the East that *you give each other* ***whatever*** *help might be required,* I got Eagle bumps up and down my neck. Maybe we're not as generous. For sure, it's a different approach to friendship.

And this plays into the differences we see in our social relationships. In the land of Dragons we tend to be more formal and hierarchal. *Quit smiling, Eagle. I know you and I aren't all that formal, but most folks in the vicinity of this great fissure will never be as candid as you and I are.* Dragons are more comfortable in the presence of a chain of command in which everyone knows his or her position...where they know what's expected of them...and where the rules and regulations are clear and relatively unchanging.

Dragon, no wonder some of my Eagle business associates go bonkers when they try to work with you. No offense, but it drives some of my colleagues crazy. Here's why. In our part of the world, informality is a way of life. We are win-win and egalitarian. Of course we have rules and boundaries, but many

也有，但許多鵰一輩子追求的就是*無拘無束*。我們稱之為*創意*…我們就是沒辦法凡事遵從上意…

鵰兄，抱歉我打個岔，但龍族的朋友，若在思想和生活上，都得如您所言這般無拘無束的話，也同樣會*發瘋*的…

…這倒也是，龍兄。我補充一下，我們的確會崇拜娛樂、體育與企業界的名人，還把他們當成偶像敬拜。老實說，連候選人在競選時，焦點都變成誰比較「受歡迎」，誰比較上鏡頭，就像高中畢業舞會結束時要選出「國王」和「皇后」一樣。可是，我們的社會已經把階級差異降到最低。或許這是因為我們的文化背景如此多元。我們是個集所有民族、語言、習俗與傳統的大熔爐。因此，為容納不同的觀點，我們必須調整思維與心態。可是，龍基本上為同一種族。你們不須要像我們一樣處理這麼多差異上的問題。

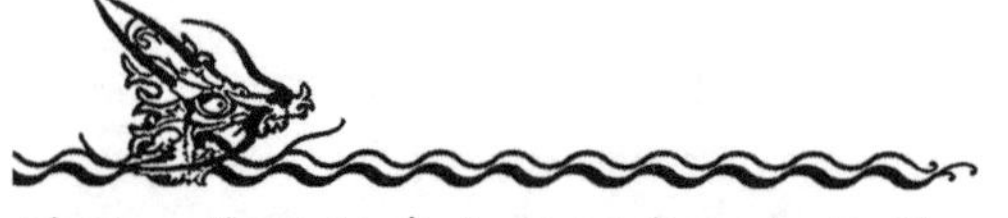

鵰兄，您的話我大致同意，但絕對不要以為「多元」的問題這兒不存在。鵰們可能覺得我們長得都一樣，但每條龍都有自己的性格、興趣和人生觀。只要到各村鎮去問大家對數百里外的同胞有什麼看法，就不難明白了。您會發現我們在習俗、飲食、方言和許多方面都不同。可是，我得同意在歷史上，我們並不是你們所稱的文化「大熔爐」。

Eagles spend their entire lives *living outside the box.* We call it being *creative*...something we don't feel we could ever do if we simply played follow the leader...

Excuse me for interrupting, Eagle, but in like manner, our Dragons would go equally *bonkers* if they had to spend their lives thinking and living outside this box you talk about...

...fair enough, Dragon. To add to what I was saying, we do tend to worship entertainment, athletic and business celebrities and place them on pedestals. In truth, our political elections have become "popularity contests," based more on media appeal, much the same as we might vote for a girl and boy in high school as "king" or "queen" of the senior prom. However social rankings in our environment are minimized. Perhaps this is because we are so culturally diverse. We are the melting pot of every nation, tongue, custom and tradition rolled into one. So we've had to adjust our thinking and our attitudes to differing points of view. You, however, are Dragons essentially of one race. You do not have to deal with diversity as much as we do.

I can't disagree with you, Eagle. But don't think for the moment that "diversity" does not exist here. We may look the same to Eagles, but each Dragon has a different personality, interest, and method of viewing life. Just go into our towns and villages and ask our Dragons what they think about their fellow citizens hundreds of miles distant. You'll find we differ in customs, foods, dialect, and much more. However, I have to agree with you that historically we are not the "melting pot" of diversity you have become.

龍兄，我完全同意。好，既然我們有許多文化議題可以討論，我想談談「義務」這個概念。我實在不太清楚你們龍族是怎麼面對這個問題的。我先說說鵰族對這個概念的看法，然後您再告訴我龍族的是否一樣。咱們鵰傾向於避免須要長期經營的關係與情況。

婚姻當然不在此列，至少半數的鵰是這麼看啦！我指的主要是一般交際與商業關係。我們就是覺得長期義務沒什麼必要。事成後離開就是了。朋友交了，還是可以說再見。我們就是好像沒法兒專注在長期的互動上。這無關對錯，但在鵰巢裡則絕對是*常態*。

唉呀，鵰兄，這種態度跟我們的人生觀非常不同。我們相信義務就是一切。收了禮，就一定要回禮。別人幫你做了筆大生意，你就必須用適當的方式回報。不回的話，風險自負。在龍的國度裡，誰幫過你的忙，你非得牢牢記住不可。當然你不用像我記得那麼久，但還真不能隨便忘記。

可是，因為我們和鵰們打交道的時間不算長，所以常忘記*鵰族仍未完全理解龍這方面的性格*。總之，和我們做生意或交往較深時，別忘了有恩報恩。鵰兄，不論您喜歡與否，都已經踏入「義務之地」中。

「義務之地」，這詞兒我喜歡。龍兄，您剛說的的確很受用。既然如此，我可以請教個相關問題嗎？這種互盡義務的概念，是否表示你們比較重人不重事？

No argument there, Dragon. Now, since we have many cultural subjects to discuss, I want to move on to the concept of "obligation." This one has me confused about how you deal with this concept in Dragonland. Let me start by stating how we regard this notion in the land of the Eagles, then you can respond with how you are the same or different. Our Eagles tend to avoid relationships and situations that demand long-term relationships.

Marriage, of course, is different—at least for half our Eagles! I'm talking here more about casual friendships and business acquaintances. We just don't feel much need for long term obligations. We do the deal, and we walk away. We make friends, and we say good bye to friends. It's like we don't have much of an attention span for enduring interaction with others. I'm not saying this is either good or bad, but it's certainly *what is* in Eagleland.

Ah, Eagle, this idea is vastly different from how we run our lives. With us, obligation is everything. You give a gift; you must return the favor with a gift. You receive assistance in landing a lucrative business contract; you must reciprocate in an appropriate way. It is at your peril not to do so. You really need a long memory in Dragon land to remember who helps you succeed in your endeavors. Perhaps not a memory as old as mine—but a long memory nonetheless.

However, since we are still relatively new in dealing with the Eagles, we often forget that *you Eagles do not yet fully understand this aspect of the Dragon personality.* Therefore, when you do business with us, or associate with us in any significant manner, be aware of your need to reciprocate for any favor offered. Like it or not, Eagle, you've entered the "obligation zone."

I like that. "The obligation zone." Yes, that is helpful indeed, Dragon. So let me ask you a related question: Does this sense of mutual obligation mean you're more relationship-oriented than task-oriented?

這個嘛…幾十年前，我會斬釘截鐵地對您說是。今天呢，則是九成肯定。儘管如此，我認為我們在商務和社交上，還是強烈地以關係為重心。當然，事情還是得做好，這從我們在工業、商業、旅遊、教育和其它方面的驚人成就，就看得出來。為了在這相對短暫的期間內完成這些目標，我們必須專注在事上，否則怎麼可能完成。

可是，我們「把事搞定」的方法，就是和身邊的朋友密切協調合作。至少對鵰來說，這可能拖延進度，但對我們來說，生活與工作相結合非常重要。

我也是這麼猜，龍兄。我們鵰認為優先順序或任務導向超越一切。關係的重要性比不上把事情做好，但目標管理和忽略信任中的人性面，也讓我們付出慘痛代價。有時候，我真的懷疑在思考和社會結構如此不同的情況下，龍與鵰怎麼可能共同完成什麼目標。

可是，鵰兄，我們的生活正因此而精彩。你們西方的某個國家是怎麼說的？*差異萬歲！*我們共有的才華，正存乎於我們的差異之中。這就是我為什麼喜歡雙贏的觀念。這麼說好了：你們到這兒來跟我們合作的時候，要意識到關係對我們的重要性。同樣的，我們到鵰巢去的時候，也要意識到*以任務為重*對你們的重要性。最棒的，討論這一切時要輕鬆以對。爭誰對誰錯沒什麼必要。鵰兄，到最後，幽默經常戰勝一切，不是嗎？

Well...a few decades ago I would have given you a clear, 100% yes to that question. Now, I'd give you a 90%. I still think we tilt strongly, however, to a relationship orientation in business and social life. Of course, we need to accomplish tasks. Witness the phenomenal growth in our industries, commerce, tourism, education, and all the rest. To accomplish these objectives in such a relatively short time period, we've had to focus on the *task* or it would not have been completed.

However, we "do the task" by working in close, harmony relationships with known Dragons in our own comfort zone. This may slow down the progress—at least in the eyes of some Eagles—but it's essentially the way we live our lives and do our work.

That was my suspicion, Dragon. With our Eagles, it's more about priority or task orientation than anything else. Relationships are not nearly as important as getting the job done, although we have paid a heavy price in managing by objectives and neglecting the human side of earning trust. You know, sometimes I wonder how Dragons and Eagles accomplish anything together given our differences in thinking and social structure.

But Eagle, this is what makes our lives interesting. How do they say it in one of your western countries? *Vive le difference!* In our dissimilarity lies our mutual genius. This is where I like your idea of win-win. Let me say it this way: when you come here to work with us, be aware of the importance of relationships to us. In like manner, when we travel to Eagleland, we need to be aware that a *task-orientation* is most important to you. Best yet, let's keep talking about all this in good humor. No one needs to be right or wrong. Humor often wins the day, don't you think, Eagle?

龍兄，您早該當心理學家才對。您一直挑難度最高的話題，然後再用滿滿的智慧加以克服。對了，我一直以為龍族沒什麼幽默感。

我們不但幽默感十足，而且還很迷信。我們迷信的，從很嚴肅的到近乎無聊的都有。

您指的是別從靠在牆上的梯子下走過，或者別讓黑貓橫越你要走的路這類東西嗎？

是的，我也知道你們會對打噴嚏的朋友說「老天保佑」，儘管這話有些怪，因為打噴嚏可能會散播細菌。至於黑貓橫越你要走的路有什麼大不了，我也搞不懂。

我們一定都有奇怪的迷信，但在我的家鄉，不管是寵物店或動物收容所，都難得用黑貓吸引家庭收養寵物。我們也盡量避免「十三」這個數字，特別是十三號星期五，連辦公大樓和飯店都幾乎沒第十三層。

我們避的是「四」，因為它在普通話和廣東話裡的發音，跟「死」這個字很接近。所以，我們的地址和電話號碼都避免有「四」。

Dragon, you should have been a psychologist. You keep taking the most challenging issues and saturate them with your wisdom. By the way, I never thought Dragons had a sense of humor.

We not only have a great sense of humor, but we are very superstitious. Our superstitions range from being very serious to being somewhat silly.

You mean like we avoid walking under a ladder leaning against a building or letting a black cat walk across the path in front of us?

Yes, and I'm aware that you say "Bless you" to a person sneezing, although that seems a bit odd, since he or she might be spreading germs. And I don't understand the significance of a black cat crossing your path.

I'm sure we both have some strange superstitions, but you'd rarely see a black cat put up for adoption by a pet store or animal shelter as a family pet where we live. We also have an aversion to the number "13," especially Friday the 13th, and our office buildings and hotels almost never have a 13th floor.

We avoid the number "4," pronounced *si* in our Putonghua and Cantonese languages, since it is similar to the character for "death." And so, we shy away from using "4" in our addresses and phone numbers.

*（忍住不笑）*呦，這還真有點兒好笑！

*（眼睛一瞪）*怎麼，您是覺得我們躲「四」沒大腦，是吧？

不，我笑的不是這個。聽見您這樣的長輩談電話號碼，實在出乎意料，讓我忍不住想笑。您洞裡的收訊怎麼樣？最喜歡哪種手機鈴聲啊？

鵬兄，您還敢笑我。我們擁有的手機數量，比西方國家的總和還多，而且我們的無線系統，跟你們那些支離破碎的老古董比起來，實在先進太多了。

是，請息怒，是我的笑話沒水準。我們不喜歡三個六連在一起，因為它不吉利，是魔鬼的象徵。我看我們別談不祥的數字，談些吉利的吧。我們很愛「七」和「十一」。

我們有很多吉祥數字。我們也喜歡「七」。我猜「一」在鵰巢裡應該很受歡迎，因為它代表著「領先」，所以我們也很喜歡。「二」也不錯，因為它象徵著兩個極端的平衡，就像陰與陽、男與女一樣。「好事成雙」是這兒很受歡迎的吉祥話。我們也喜歡「五」，因為我們有五行和五吉。「六」也很好，因為它跟「祿」的發音很接近。

*(suppressing a chuckle)* Oh, that strikes me as funny!

*(glaring)* Do you mean we are ill-advised for shunning the number "4"?

No, not because of that. It just tickles me that someone as ancient and unlikely as you would talk about telephone numbers. What kind of reception do you get in your cave? What are your favorite ring tones?

Don't mock me, Eagle. We have more cell phones than the rest of the Western countries combined, and our wireless systems are more advanced than your rather piecemeal, antiquated set-ups.

Okay, already. I made a bad joke. We don't like the numbers "666," because they represent a bad omen as the sign of evil. But let's get off the subject of bad numbers and go for the lucky ones. We love "7" and "11."

We have many lucky numbers. We also like the number "7." The number "1," which I assume is very popular in Eagleland, because it portends "leadership," is also popular with us. The number "2" is good because it symbolizes the balance between two opposite poles, such as the *yin* and *yang*, man and woman. A popular saying here is "Happiness comes in twos." We also like the number "5" because of our Five Elements Philosophy and our five major blessings. The number "6" is good because it is similar to the word "wealth" in our language.

這可比我們多很多。你們最幸運的數字是什麼？

第一次見面時，我就說過「九」是最受尊重的。龍共有九種，由不同動物的部位所組成，且「九」象徵著成就的顛峰。我記得「九」在古代只有皇帝可以使用。如果裁縫在給客人的長袍上繡了九條龍，不但他自己人頭不保，還會被滿門抄斬

原來在那個時代，顯然只有皇帝和他的御用裁縫，才覺得「九」是幸運數字吧！

那是好幾百年前的事了，但甚至在今天，我認為「八」是大家最喜歡的數字之一。某個省的某位大富商，幾年前為了得到一個結尾是五個「八」的電話號碼，花了相當於二萬五千美元。

您真是愛說笑！

是真的。「八」在我們的語言裡聽起來像「發」，也就是繁榮的意思。此外，「八」在幾何上代表著八邊形，等同於帶有八個角的八卦，是個很吉利的形狀，常用來保護風水。

That's a lot more than we have. What about your luckiest numbers?

As I said the first time we met, "9" is revered. There are nine of my kind, made up of nine different animal parts, and "9" stands for the ultimate fulfillment. I recall that in ancient times the number "9" was considered to be the sole preserve of the emperor. If a tailor made a robe with "9" Dragons on it for anyone else, he would be executed along with all of his relatives.

In those days, the number "9" apparently was only lucky for the emperor and his private tailor!

That was many, many centuries ago. But even today, I would say that one of our most favored numbers is the number "8." A few years ago, a prominent business man in one of our provinces paid more than 25,000 of your dollars for a phone number ending with five "8's."

You're joking!

Not at all. The number "8" sounds like "multiply" in our language. The pronunciation of "8" is *ba* which sounds similar to *fa,* the Chinese character for prosperity. And, geometrically, it is the octagon, or the eight pointed *baqua,* a very auspicious shape often used in *feng shui* for protection.

*（來回踱步）*好，龍兄，先停一下。您又讓我聽不懂了。我瞭解「八」受歡迎的程度，而且仔細想想，難怪有這麼多龍會在我國特定的郊區買房子，因為那兒的郵遞區號裡有很多「八」，以及他們為什麼都喜歡開頭是「八八八」的免付費電話。

沒錯。那您究竟是哪兒不懂？

那個八邊形的東西，以及好*「風水」*的概念。在我們今天的文化裡，八邊形讓人想起的是有八個面的大圍籠，所謂的「終極戰士」在裡面互相痛毆，互掐脖子直到對手認輸為止，好取悅四周買票入場的觀眾。

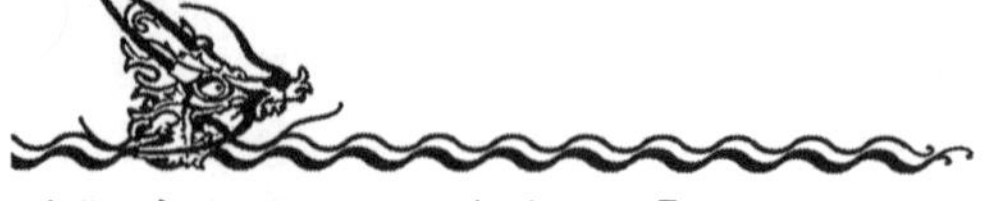

聽起來很粗暴，簡直是「黷武之術」！

說得好，龍兄。我們在娛樂方面的品味有點兒退步了，這些應該是羅馬全盛時期菁英們才喜歡的玩意兒。可是，您剛一提*「風水」*，我就有點兒措手不及了。

我的舊「羽」新知啊，我還以為您很懂*風水*。*風水*在西方的上流文化裡似乎是股熱潮。

*(pacing back and forth)* Now, hold on, Dragon. You're losing me again. I understand that "8" is a prized number, and now that I think of that, it is no longer a mystery why so many of your Dragons have purchased homes in certain of our suburbs, with area codes that sport many "8's" and also why they seek toll free numbers that have the prefix "888."

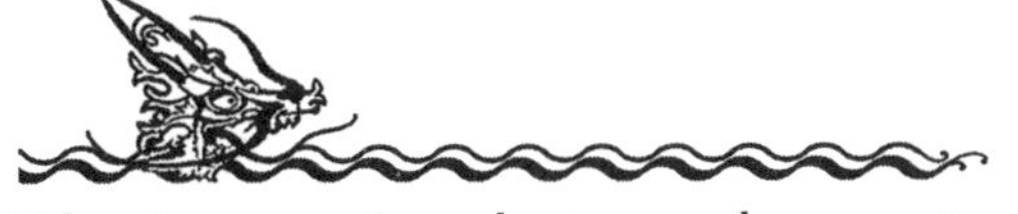

That's true. So what puzzles you?

It's that octagon stuff and good *"feng shui."* The octagon in our current culture is a caged arena where what we call "ultimate fighters" beat each other senseless or choke each other into submission to the delight of paid audiences.

Sounds vulgar to me, like "unmartialed arts!"

Well said, Dragon. We're moving a bit backward in our entertainment tastes, which would have appealed to the Roman elite at the peak of their civilization. But you threw me a curve when you added the *"feng shui"* reference.

I certainly expected you to be up on *feng shui,* my fine feathered friend. It seems to be the rage in your upscale Western culture.

我只知道風水像是種「建築針灸」，只要花大錢讓大門和家具面對某個方向就能「避邪」。

您有時似乎很天真，但我猜是因為您的年紀太輕，不太會解讀風俗習慣。*風水*的字面意義就是風與水，是一種古代的大自然哲學，精神在於怎麼與自然*共存*，而不是對抗。如果我們周遭盡是吵雜與喧鬧，只會冷眼看待生命和自然，步上衰亡之路是必然的。可是，如果我們擁抱美麗、溫柔、悅耳的音樂及生命散發的自然芳香，就能使自己和環境日益高尚。

我們相信，真正的*風水*師不但熟悉金、木、水、火、土等五行之道，也對「氣」的流動非常敏銳，可為客戶的建築、裝潢和景觀營造綜合效應，與自然協調一致。這對我們的文化來說是很基本的。

好，我們之間的友好關係，似乎就有好*風水*的加持。我們可以開始談談比較輕鬆的異同之處了。過年的方式怎麼樣？龍族會在午夜倒數，然後開香檳慶祝嗎？

我們過年既熱鬧又傳統。慶祝是從初一的新月開始，到十五的滿月

All I know is that it's some kind of "architectural acupuncture," where you pay a lot of money to face your doors and furniture in a certain direction to ward off bad "mojo."

Sometimes you seem so naïve, but I suppose it's because you are so young when it comes to understanding customs. *Feng shui* (pronounced "phung schwee")—meaning, literally, "wind water"—is part of an ancient philosophy of nature. It is about living *with* rather than *against* the natural environment. If we surround ourselves with discord, noise and indifference toward life and nature, we will corrupt ourselves in the process. However, if we embrace beauty, gentleness, lovely music and natural expressions of the sweet aroma of life, we ennoble ourselves as well as our environment.

We believe that legitimate *feng shui* masters not only understand our ancient Five Elements Philosophy, or the relationship between water, gold, wood, fire and earth, but also have a special sense for the flow of what we call *chi* energy to help their clients create synergy in their buildings, furnishings and landscapes to harmonize with nature. It's basic to our culture.

Well you and I seem to have pretty good *feng shui* in our rapport, so let's move on to some lighter topics concerning our similarities and differences. What about celebrations like welcoming in the New Year? Do Dragons count down to midnight and let the champagne flow?

Our New Year celebrations are very festive and full of tradition. Our annual event starts with the new moon on the first day of the New Year and ends on the full moon 15 days later. Although, be-

結束。可是，現代社會的步調又快又忙，許多朋友只有七天的時間慶祝。可是，那段時間裡，慶祝可是日夜不停的。

哇，若是我們，一定會有很多朋友請病假。

年初十五是「元宵節」，入夜後有花燈展示，以及孩子們提燈籠遊街。初一到十五，天天都有特別的慶祝方式。唯一不變的，是我們在那兩星期吃下肚的，比剩下的五十個星期還多！

你們的新年新志向，一定是減肥啦！

新年新志向？

是，我們年底時都會寫下許多新志向，像是控制飲食、多多運動、把債還清等等，但二月一日，也就是大概一個月後，我們就認真把這些志向忘得一乾二淨。

看樣子你們「除舊佈新」的方法，真是虛晃一招而已。可是，我喜歡這種在新年排定優先順序的觀念。沒有目標的話，我們簡直就像沒羅盤的船一樣。

cause of our busy schedules in this fast-forward world, many in our culture can only afford to celebrate for about a week. But we celebrate day and night during that time.

Wow, that would make a lot of our workers have to take sick leave from their jobs.

The 15th day of the New Year is called the "lantern festival," which is held at night with lantern displays and children carrying lanterns in a parade. And each of the 15 days is celebrated in a special way. About the only thing in common is that we consume more food during those two weeks than in the remaining fifty weeks of the year!

Your main New Year's resolutions must focus on dieting!

New Year's resolutions?

Yes, those involve a list of promises we make at the end of the year, such as eating and drinking less, exercising more and getting out of debt, that we proceed to break religiously by February 1st of the same New Year, about a month later.

You sound as if you take a more frivolous approach to "sweeping out" the old and welcoming in the new. But I like the notion of a list of priorities for the New Year. Without clear goals, we simply are like ships without compasses.

在我們的歷史早期，過年比較著重在家庭與摯友上，而不只是找群人大肆狂歡，第二天整天看足球，試著恢復前晚耗盡的體力而已。我比較喜歡自我反省過去一年的成就、挑戰與幸福，並積極歡迎一個嶄新的開始。

我們滿重視過年的傳統。除夕前房子要打掃乾淨，債也要還清，好把過去的一年「掃」出門。除夕和初一著重在家人同歡，是團圓與感恩的時刻。

我猜你們的過年，結合了我們的感恩節、夏季團圓和除夕。每年十一月，我們都與家人享用大餐，慶祝自己有幸活在富足的土地上。我們通常會在夏天全家團圓，因為此時許多人都能放一個星期左右的假。我們和龍族不一樣，大多住得離父母與長輩很遠，能見面的機會不多。

我們在除夕有個傳統，就是吃年夜飯時為祖先留位子，表達我們對他們的思念與尊敬。這頓大餐又叫「圍爐」，象徵全家團圓，不僅表示對這一代的尊重，也紀念那些為家財和家業奠定根基的已逝親人。

Early in our history, our New Year's celebrations used to be more focused on family and best friends, rather than just having one grand party with a crowd and watching football games all the next day, trying to recover from the night before. I much prefer an intimate reflection on the accomplishments, challenges, and blessings of the old year, and a positive welcoming of a fresh, new beginning.

We take our New Year tradition quite seriously. Prior to New Year's Eve all the housecleaning should be completed, and debts paid, to "sweep" out the old year. New Year's Eve and New Year's Day are celebrated as a family affair, a time of reunion and thanksgiving.

I guess your New Year's events are like our Thanksgiving Day, summer family reunions and New Year's Eve celebrations combined. We celebrate our family and thankfulness for living in such an abundant land every November with a large feast. We usually have family reunions in the summer, when many of us can take a week or so off from our work. Unlike you Dragons, most of us Eagles live far away from our parents and elders, and probably don't see each other as often.

On New Year's Eve we have a tradition of remembering and respecting our ancestors with a dinner arranged for them at the family banquet table. This feast is called "surrounding the stove" or *weilu*. It symbolizes family unity and honors the present generation, along with those departed relatives who laid the foundation for the fortune and glory of our family.

這點子真不錯，龍兄。我就希望把這種觀念注入鵰的家庭。今天的孩子大多與祖父母或親戚沒什麼感情，多半也不知道曾祖父母是誰，是怎麼過完一生的。龍族正在這個步調快速的世界裡力爭上游，不知道您最喜歡的傳統，以後是不是能傳承下去。

*（嘆氣）*我希望我們在現代化的同時，也能留住先人的豐富傳統。我真的很高興你我雖然如此不同，還能不帶敵意地暢談。敢問鵰族是怎麼處理批判、挑釁且有爭議的話題？我在這方面經驗不足，所以必須瞭解鵰的觀點。

答案很簡單。鵰族在家鄉做生意的時候，喜歡直接衝突。我們不在意同時批判許多不同的觀點。我們試著以禮相待，但絕不會不敢表達最不同或甚至激進的看法，爭議性再高也在所不惜。

我們有雜誌、電子報、報紙、部落格、全天候有線電視，應有盡有。任何年齡、尺寸或大小的鵰，都可以盡情說出他們心中的「真相」。我們甚至有家運動用品公司，口號居然是*做就是了！*（注意，不是優雅、溫柔、關懷或熱心地去「做」）反正就是*先做再說！*

What a great idea, Dragon. That's certainly one I'd like to instill in our Eagle families. Too often, today, many of our children have no relationship with grandparents or extended family members, and most of them have no idea who their great-grandparents were, or how they lived. I wonder if you'll be able to carry on your favorite traditions as you move upward and outward in this fast-forward world.

*(sighing)* I hope we can modernize without losing the rich connection with our heritage. I appreciate the fact that although you and I are so different, we have been able to converse without really taking offense to the other's opinions. How do you Eagles deal with criticism, confrontation and controversial topics? I don't have a lot of experience in this area, so I need to understand this from an Eagle's point of view.

That's an easy question to answer. When doing business in Eagle land with each other, we enjoy direct confrontation. We are comfortable with critiquing many differing points of view—often at the same time. We try to do it in a civilized manner, but that doesn't stop us from expressing our most diverse—even radical—opinions, no matter how controversial they might be.

We have magazines, ezines, newspapers, blogs, 24-hour cable news—you name it—in which Eagles of all ages, shapes and sizes continually express their opinions about what they consider to be "the truth." We even have a sports company that has the slogan *Just Do It!* (Notice, they don't say "do it" with grace, kindness, love or compassion. It's *Just Do It!* )

鵬兄，這對我們來說很難，真的很難。不瞞您說，我們認為「保住面子」就等於保命。我們不喜歡直接衝突。我們避免相互公開批評。沒有一條龍喜歡被冷落在角落。太丟臉了。這就是為什麼爭議性的話題，大家避而不談。我們在做人處事上盡力做根竹子，就像國畫中常見的溪水一樣順勢而為。我們順著自然的意思過生活。

所以，鵬兄，你們過來做生意、讀書或四處旅遊的時候，務必要把批判的心態擱在一旁，知道什麼時候該給我們留面子。做不到的話，會把自己、事業和人際關係都毀了。相信我準沒錯。

*（鼓鼓翅膀）*龍兄，我對您的信任，絕對超乎您的想像。*（仰頭望天）*老大哥，上頭的天氣越來越糟，我也該回去了。可是，我認為今天的交流結束之前，我們已經討論過最重要的話題：那就是該如何尊重對方的感覺，同時不傷及彼此的感情。我再次強調，只要持續嘗試溝通，我們共同的未來就越美好越富足。啊，對了，我可以預見龍與鵬的合作長長久久。

夜已降臨，風雨蓄勢待發。鵬離開朋友返回鵬巢的時候已到。鵬用力一拍翅膀，就飛向快速變黑的天空中…但他已學到更多，也準備好把今天所學與其他鵬分享。

冬天將至，而鵬也知道不久後，雪雨交加會阻礙視線，讓他無法飛行，地面的大岩縫屆時也將被大雪覆蓋。這讓他更加珍惜過去幾個月所學，並不斷默記龍所說過的一切來提醒自己，同時希望還能跟這位老朋友至少再見兩次面。

That's tough for us, Eagle. Really tough. You see, for us "saving face" is life itself. We dislike direct confrontation. We avoid open criticism of one another. No Dragon appreciates being shoved into a corner. It's embarrassing. That's why contentious topics are kept under wraps. In our relationships with each other we do our best to bend like the bamboo and flow like the stream that's depicted in our many artistic paintings. We take our cues from nature and we live accordingly.

So Eagle, when you work with us, study with us or travel in our vast region, you simply must put your own idea of criticism aside and be sensitive to our need to save face. Not to do this will be catastrophic for you, your business and your relationships with our Dragons. Trust me.

*(puffing its wings)* I do trust you, Dragon, more than you realize. My friend *(looking skyward)*, it's getting stormy up there and I think I'd better head home. However, I think we've ended today's exchange on one of the most important topics of all: how to respect each other's feelings without doing damage to Dragon or Eagle sensibilities. Again, as long as we keep trying to understand each other, the better and more productive our future together will be. And, by the way, I see Dragons and Eagles working together for decades to come.

Night had now fallen and a storm was brewing. It was time for Eagle to leave its friend and return to the land of the Eagles. With one forceful lifting of its wings, Eagle quickly ascended into the fast darkening skies...better informed and prepared to share what it had learned today with other Eagles.

Winter was fast approaching and Eagle knew it would not be able to fly in the blinding sleet and snow that would soon cover the great fissure in the earth. So it savored what it had learned over the past months, continually making mental notes of all Dragon had said—all the time hoping there would be at least two more encounters with its ancient friend.

# 摘要

第五回

# Summary

CHAPTER 5

## 文化挑戰

## Cultural Challenges

# 龍親口告訴我們…
# *Straight from the Dragon's mouth...*

☯ 若您覺得我們有天會成為自吹自擂的專家，就大錯特錯了。我們的天性就是融入，服從上層的命令，遵循社會規範。

☯ 注意看我們怎麼互動，觀察龍族間的友誼。不論如何，我們絕對都比較信任龍，而非偶爾掠過的鵰。鵰兄，很抱歉…本性難移。

☯ If you think we'll ever become accomplished at "tooting our own horn" you're mistaken. Our basic nature is to fit in, be obedient to those in charge, and cooperate with society's norms.

☯ Pay attention to how we engage each other. Check out our friendships here in Dragon land. Like it or not, we will always trust our own Dragons more than we'll ever trust the Eagles who do their fly-bys. Sorry, Eagle... that's just the way it is.

## 鵰的看法則是…

## *From the Eagle's point of view...*

✶ 鵰熱愛自立與自我推銷帶來的快感。正是這種快感，使開發人類潛能的訓練蔚為風潮。我們拒絕受限於傳統。我們受不了傳統。

✶ 龍與鵰合作時，務必要瞭解雙方對友誼的看法不同。我們認為友誼有限。我們不依靠彼此之間長期的義務。我們的朋友多，但交情深的很少。龍兄，這個問題有待我們解決。

✶ Eagles love the excitement of self-reliance and self-promotion. In fact, the human potential seminar movement relies on our need for this. We refuse to be boxed in by tradition. It drives us crazy.

✶ When Dragons work with Eagles, it's important to realize we're different from each other when it comes to our view of friendships. We see friendships as limited. We do not rely on mutual obligations long term. We have many friends and few intimates. We'll just have to work this out, Dragon.

# 龍親口告訴我們…
# *Straight from the Dragon's mouth...*

☯ 絕不要以為各位能改變我們對「職權」的看法。我們對自己的指揮體系很滿意。每條龍都知道自己的位置時，大家的表現就比較順暢。我們要他人知道我們的職責，這樣工作與生活時才覺得有所依循。我們選擇不要「有創意地」合作。

☯ Please do not think for a moment that you can change our view of "position." We like our chain of command. We function better when every Dragon knows his or her status. We want others to know what's expected of us—and then we feel we can live and work accordingly. We don't choose to operate "outside the box."

## 鵬的看法則是…

# From the Eagle's point of view...

✳ 不拘禮節和自我表現，在西方是很正常的。若龍族的朋友不瞭解這一點，永遠會覺得無所適從。我們討厭「遵從上意」。沒錯，我們最喜歡無拘無束的生活，因為這是最佳創意的泉源。然而，團隊合作上，我們絕對有改善的空間，並用合作調節競爭。

✳ In the West, informality and self-expression are a way of life. If those in Dragonland do not understand this, there will be non-stop confusion. We hate to play "follow the leader." Yes, we love living outside the box because that's where our best and most creative ideas lie. However, we certainly can improve our teamwork and balance competition, with more cooperation.

# 龍親口告訴我們…
# Straight from the Dragon's mouth...

☯ 若您或您的公司不瞭解龍族對「義務」的看法，就會覺得龍地處處是阻礙。互惠是最基本的原則。別忘記誰對您有恩，然後用心回報。做不到的話，您就只能唱獨腳戲，搞不清楚哪兒出了問題。

☯ If you or your company does not understand the Dragon view of "obligation," you'll have great difficulty working in Dragonland. Reciprocity is the order of the day. Always remember who brought you to the dance—and then reward that person in a significant way. If you don't do this, you'll be sitting alone at the table, wondering what you did wrong.

## 鵰的看法則是…
## *From the Eagle's point of view...*

✶ 生意做成時，我們會感激他人的協助。然而，鵰不會把龍眼中的「義務」發揮到極致。老實說，我們傾向於避免長期的關係和情勢，*除非商業上的理由非常充足*。大多數時候，我們生意做完就走，除非這筆生意還有後續的商機。我們不會跳入龍眼中的「義務範圍」裡。

✶ We're grateful for assistance when we put together a business deal. However, Eagles don't take the Dragons' sense of "obligation" to the extreme. In fact, we tend to avoid long-term relationships and situations *unless there is a strong business reason not to.* For the most part, we do the deal and walk away—unless the "deal" has spawned other opportunities to engage in business. We don't get stuck in what Dragon calls "the obligation zone."

# 龍親口告訴我們…

# *Straight from the Dragon's mouth...*

☯ 千萬別以為龍對「任務」的重視，高於「完成」任務所需的關係。為了把工作做好，我們會與同事保持和諧，即使流於表面也是如此。我們不會忘記事情是誰做的，為什麼要做和什麼時候做的。記憶力強很有用，筆記做得好也有幫助！

☯ Never think that the Dragon's "task" orientation is more important than the vital relationships needed to "accomplish" the task. Even if it is surface in nature, we work in close harmony with other Dragons to get the job done. We always remember who did what, why and when. It helps to have a long memory. It also helps to take good notes!

# 鵰的看法則是…

# *From the Eagle's point of view...*

✶ 鵰比較注重的，是任務不是關係。我們就像東方的朋友一樣，需要同事幫忙把工作做好。可是，同事隨時能換，反正一定有別的鵰隨「翅」在側，好把任務完成。我剛有些俏皮，請別介意。只要有目標，我們就能拿出計畫完成它，有沒有長期關係都無所謂。為了完成任務，我們重視的是技能，而非友誼。然而，邊試邊學，也讓我們瞭解到互信與團隊精神，才能決定我們在全球市場上的成就與領導地位。

✶ Eagles are more focused on tasks than relationships. We, like those in the East, need to have our colleagues on hand to help us get the job done. But these Eagles are expendable. That's because there are always other Eagles waiting in the wings, if you'll excuse the pun, to get the job done. Show us the objective, and we'll come up with a plan to get it done—with or without long-term friendships. We favor skilled participants more than friends to help us accomplish a task. However, we have learned by trial and error that mutual trust and teamwork will determine our ability to lead and succeed in the global marketplace.

# 龍親口告訴我們…
# *Straight from the Dragon's mouth...*

☯ 鵰有時候可能會覺得我們很迷信，甚至迷信得令人不解或啼笑皆非。然而，這就是我們的生活方式，而且已持續好幾千年，是龍族很重要的一部份。所以，多給我們「八」，少給我們「四」。請遷就我們對**風水**的執著。鵰只要能瞭解這一古老習俗，就能讓我們相信您是誠心想認識東方的居民。不要嘲笑我們。我們對這些迷信很認真，因為其中有些涉及我們想永久保存的珍貴傳統。

☯ Sometimes Eagles may think it strange—or even amusing—that we are so superstitious. But that's the way we live, and it's been that way for many millennia. It's a critical element in our make-up. So give us lots of "8's" and very few "4's." Indulge us in our belief in ***feng shui***. An Eagle's simple awareness of this facet of our ancient culture tells us you're serious about getting to know the inhabitants of the East. But don't laugh at us. We take these superstitions seriously, because some of them involve cherished traditions we never want to abandon.

# 鵰的看法則是…

# From the Eagle's point of view...

✱ 西方也有自己的迷信。然而，我們不像龍族的朋友一樣，讓迷信左右著自己的生活。我們對數字沒那麼認真，其實還常拿「十三」開玩笑。我們對*風水*也沒這麼感興趣。鵰族的土地開發商，想建哪裡就建哪裡，想向哪裡就向哪裡，蓋房子時也不多考慮它在環境裡「與自然的平衡」。對龍與鵰而言，這沒什麼誰對誰錯的問題。我們只不過必須瞭解*並接納*這些彼此之間的小細節。然而，有句話我得告訴各位：我們用以驅除霉運的，是辛勤有紀律地工作，而非門或窗的位置。

✱ The West also has its share of superstitions. However, we don't allow them to rule our lives to the same extent as our Dragonland friends. We certainly don't take numbers all that seriously—and, in fact, we pretty much joke about the number 13. We just don't get energized about *feng shui.* Our Eagleland contractors will build anywhere, face any direction they please, and construct dwellings in any environment without a lot of concern for "nature's balance." Neither Dragons nor Eagles are right or wrong here. It's simply important for us to know *and accept* these details about each other. However, I must say this: we banish bad mojo by hard, disciplined work, not through the careful positioning of a door or window.

# 龍親口告訴我們…
# Straight from the Dragon's mouth...

☯ 批評、衝突與爭議性的話題，是龍族的禁忌。別以為「下班後」，您的龍族朋友就不會介意這些行為。不好衝突是我們的天性，所以別讓我們感到不自在。否則，我們會面紅耳赤，開始流汗，顯得渾身不舒服。最後，我們會送您到門口。一切到此為止。然而，鵰兄，我們不希望如此，所以雙方的對話絕不能斷。

☯ Criticism, confrontation and controversial topics are taboo in Dragonland. And don't think you can get away with adopting these attitudes "after hours" with Dragons you assume you can trust. It's in our DNA ***not*** to confront. So don't make us uncomfortable. If you do, we'll get red in the face. We'll start sweating. We'll exhibit enormous discomfort. Lastly, we'll walk you to the door. End of story. But we don't want to do this, Eagle. So let's keep talking.

## 鵬的看法則是…

## *From the Eagle's point of view...*

✢ 西方很愛爭議。太陽底下的任何東西，我們都可以拿來辯論、討論和爭論。不論是政治、宗教、運動或商業，只要叫得出名字的，我們就有辦法辨。這是*我們的*天性，也反映在我們能自由參與這些活動上。我們珍惜不同的論點，並從中擷取活力。龍兄，這就是我們的相處之道。可是，我們在龍地工作、玩樂和讀書時，會盡量不那麼愛辯！

✢ In the West we love controversy. We debate, discuss and argue every point of view under the sun: politics, religion, sports, and business—you name it. This is part of *our* DNA, and we revel in the freedom to engage in these activities. We value—and receive energy from—the diversity of many points of view. Dragon, this is how we are with each other. But we will do our best to tone down the rhetoric while we work, play and study in Dragonland!

第六回

CHAPTER 6

# 心智王國

# Empires of the Mind

這對原本不太可能成為朋友的朋友，有個特別的話題要談。某個嚴寒的清晨，鵬一抵達東方，龍就用溫暖的茉莉花茶和熊熊柴火接待，讓鵬覺得很窩心。現在唯一冰冷的，是戶外的空氣，因為透過交流，雙方得以瞭解並尊重彼此的差異，使他們打從骨子裡感覺暖烘烘的。不過，他們也承認彼此的瞭解仍然很淺。

他們相信對方也熱切地想分享學習，且不抱成見，因此同意討論「知識時代」這個深遠的新千禧年議題。之前會面時，他們已經觸及教育的重要性，以及將智慧傳承給後代的必要性。鵬覺得龍對這個主題的看法一定最有道理，龍也期待獲得全新的靈感與宏大的觀點，以面對這個不斷進步的世界，因為其中唯一不變的，就是改變。

龍兄，好一堆火。這真是最適合深入討論的環境。

這個嘛，我們到目前為止都還處得不錯，因為我們都願意自曝其短，同時不會因彼此的成見而謾罵。

跟您見面後，我覺得這真的很重要。如果我承認自己的短處，您就比較願意跟我分享。

這個世界需要少些隨口的批評，多些願意挺身解決問題的好手。古代哲人老子備受我們所推崇，而他寫的道德經教人如何自助，是我最喜歡的經典之一。老子就常說：「知人者智，知己者明。」我們

This was to be a special session between the unlikely friends. As the Eagle appeared in the East on a frosty morning, it appreciated the hot cup of jasmine tea and the fire that the Dragon had prepared. The only chill was in the outside air, for, by now, the dialogue between the two, which fostered understanding of and respect for their differences, had created a warmth in the very marrow of their bones. They both acknowledged how little they still really knew about each other.

Trusting that each was eager to share and learn, without pre-judgment, they had agreed to discuss the all-encompassing subject of the new millennium being called "The Knowledge Era." In previous meetings they had touched on the importance of education and the critical need to pass on the wisdom of the ages to each succeeding generation. The Eagle sensed that the Dragon would have the best perspective on the subject, while the Dragon anticipated gaining some fresh ideas and a broader view of a fast-forward world, where the only rule is change.

Nice fire, Dragon. Perfect environment for an in-depth discussion.

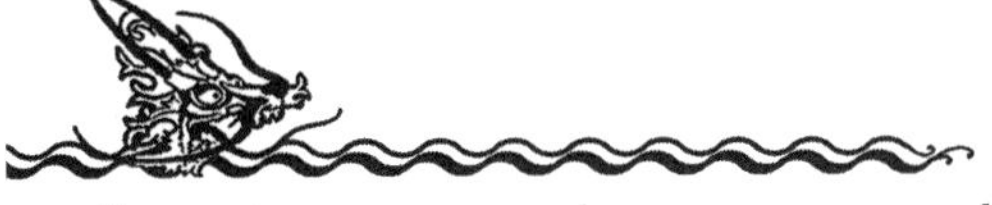

Well, we've gotten along pretty well so far, since we both volunteer our own shortcomings, without insulting the other's bias.

That's something important I've learned after meeting you. If I admit my own shortcomings, you're more vulnerable to share yours with me.

The world needs fewer sideline critics and more players willing to step into the arena and participate in the solutions. Our revered, ancient philosopher, Lao Tzu, who wrote the *Tao Te Ching*—one of my favorite self-help books—often said "To know others is intelligence; to know myself is wisdom." Each of us must look in the

都應該看看鏡子，就會知道誰該為自己的成敗負責。我們必須成為一輩子的學生和領導，因為唯命是從者，只會眼睜睜地被進步所淘汰。在這個嶄新的全球格局中，唯有明智者，才能夠有主導權。無知所造成的欺虐與奴役，將更甚於過去。

二次大戰結束時，我們上世紀最傑出的盟友之一邱吉爾曾說過：「未來的王國，不是用石頭、槍砲和軍隊所建造的。未來的王國，將會是心智的王國。」

他的觀察真是一語中的。很不幸的，數個世紀以來，我們有許多帝王和朝代，都是靠武力而起，但也因暴虐而亡。過去，勝利就等於爭權奪位，通常意味以勝利者的姿態，踩在戰死的敵人或對手身上。

但這再也行不通了，不是嗎？未來的領袖應該倡導合作，而不是競爭。

我同意。擁有維繫生活的資源固然重要，但適者生存的心態終將被淘汰，起而代之的將是智者生存，一種整合理解、合作、知識與理性的哲學理念。真正的領袖，將透過滿足他人而滿足自我。不好意思，我要再次引用老子的話：「悠兮其貴言。功成事遂，百姓皆謂：『*我自然。*』」

mirror to see who is responsible for our success or failure. We must become lifelong learners and leaders, for to be followers today is to fall hopelessly behind the pace of progress. The power brokers in the new global arena will be the knowledge facilitators. Ignorance will be even more the tyrant and enslaver than in the past.

At the end of World War II, Winston Churchill—one of our most prominent allies of the past century—said that "the empires of the future will not be built of stone, with turrets and armies. The empires of the future will be empires of the mind."

How prophetic that observation was. Sadly, many of our empires and dynasties in centuries past have risen by the sword and fallen upon it. Winning used to center around power and being number one. It often meant standing victoriously over a fallen adversary or competitor.

But that idea won't work any longer, will it? The leaders of tomorrow should be more the champions of cooperation, rather than champions of competition.

I believe that. While maintaining access to life-sustaining resources will remain critical, the "survival of the fittest" mentality will give way to survival of the wisest, a philosophy of understanding, cooperation, knowledge and reason. The authentic leaders will get what they want by helping others get what they want. Again, you'll pardon me if I quote Lao Tzu again: "A leader is best when people barely know he exists. When his work is done, his aim fulfilled, they will say: *'We did it ourselves.'*"

我們在觀察龍族與您的鄰國印度時，發現今天的世界人口太多但資源過少，自然與科技間又難以平衡，領袖們再也不能靠關門閉戶解決問題。除非「大家都分得到餅」，否則和平將無法持續。

這就是為什麼我們要的是努力，不是爭鬥。相信明天的餅會變大變好，且大家都能多分一些，就不用再為今天的餅該怎麼分而拼死拼活。龍與鵰都必須知道，若把全球的人口視為身體，我們雙方就是那個最關鍵的器官。任何一個群體，都必須仰賴全體，才可能成功，甚至生存下去。一心想報數世紀前的舊仇，或者因宗教信仰而衝突，注定帶來毀滅。偏見與無知其實是一體兩面。

在鵰族裡，中上階級吃飽了以後，就開始追求娛樂與休閒。可是在落後國家裡，因為吃不飽，所以一切決定與行為都是為了趕快吃飽。動機是引發行為的那股內在力量。我們幾乎是一眨眼，就從農業文化轉型成製造文化，並正快速邁向科技文化。我們瞭解知識和訊息，是機會和進步的關鍵。

*（高興地拍動雙翼）*哇！好棒的觀念。您到我國競選的話，什麼都選得上。您的思維令我激賞，口才更是驚人。是誰說大型爬蟲類很笨的啊？

When we observe your Dragon population, and that of your neighbors in India, we realize that the world now has too many people, too few resources, and too delicate a balance between nature and technology for leaders to operate in isolation. I don't see how we can have lasting peace until there's a "piece of pie in every mouth."

That's why we toil instead of fight. The expectation of tomorrow's bigger, better pie, of which everyone will enjoy a larger piece, is what prevents people from struggling to the end over the division of today's pie. We Dragons and Eagles must acknowledge that we are a vital but single organ of the larger body of the world's population. One segment of human beings can no longer succeed—perhaps even survive—without the others. Seeking revenge from centuries' old misdeeds or clashing over differences in religious beliefs are prescriptions for annihilation. Prejudice and ignorance are one in the same.

When the belly is full, as with your middle and upper class Eagles, entertainment and diversion become the goals. When the belly is empty, as in the under-developed nations, people need to think and act with urgency in order to eat. Motivation is an inner force that compels behavior. In almost the blink of an eye, our own society is being transformed from an agrarian culture to a manufacturing culture, and rapidly moving toward a technology-driven culture. We understand that knowledge and information are the keys to opportunity and advancement.

*(flapping its wings enthusiastically)* Wow! What a great concept. You could win any election you ran for in my country. I really like the way you think and I marvel at your oratory skills. Whoever said big reptiles were not supposed to be bright?

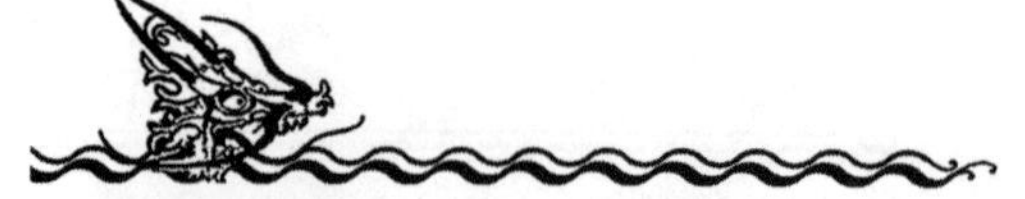

*（鼻子噴氣）*我可不是爬蟲。我們一開始談的，您這麼快就忘了嗎？我集九種不同的動物於一身。你的祖先才是會飛的爬蟲，鵰兄，而且我叫您「笨鳥」過嗎？叫過嗎？

*（雙翼交叉微笑）*我不過是想在我們的談話裡加點料而已。我們的話題過於嚴肅，搞得我頭都痛了。

我們倆都需要新鮮空氣。我想帶您飛到一些市區和鄉下看看。您應該知道我沒翅膀也能飛，對吧？

您現在不管說什麼還是做什麼，我都不會覺得奇怪了。打從我們認識的頭一天開始，您就不斷讓我赫然發現*「原來如此」*！

外頭挺涼的，但沒什麼雲，而且我們如果飛得夠快，身體大概就會暖活舒服些。快跟上。

*(snorting)* I'm not a reptile. Have you forgotten so soon about our initial conversation? I'm the embodiment of nine different animals. Your ancestors were flying reptiles, Eagle, and you haven't heard me refer to you once as "bird-brain," now have you?

*(crossing its wings and smiling)* I just wanted to add a little levity in our discussion. We're getting into such serious stuff that I'm starting to get a headache.

What we both need is some fresh air. I'm going to take you on a brief tour of some of our cities and rural terrain by air. You were aware that I could fly, even without wings, weren't you?

Nothing you could say or do would surprise me at this point. You have been full of *"ah-ha!"* revelations for me since the day we met.

It's pretty cold outside, but there are no clouds, and if we fly fast we'll generate enough heat to stay comfortable. Follow me.

話一說完，龍就領著鵰升空，然後以緊密隊形快速地從高度發達的沿海城市，飛向中部與西部等較落後的工業與農業地區。古今相融的強烈對比，讓鵰目瞪口呆：繁榮的城市與工廠旁，就是古老的洞穴，以及老舊的房屋和披屋；媲美西方的最現代化高速公路，朝四面八方延伸，但附近城鎮裡的小路與街道，卻塵土飛揚凹凸不平；農事多在小塊的農地上進行，耕耘和收割多以手工完成；太空時代的科技，與銅器時代的生態共存。然而，最令人驚訝的，是數量龐大的貨車、公交車、火車、自行車、汽車與推車，以及成千萬成百萬的行人，全部只朝一個方向前進：在廿一世紀的宴席上，努力贏得一席之地。

*（上氣不接下氣）*等等，龍兄。您沒翅膀要揮動，但我有。我一直在數我們飛過了幾所大學。光是北京市的大學數，就比我們許多州還多！剛見面時的談話裡，你曾提到你們的大學應屆畢業生人數，是我們的四倍。

*（向鵰靠攏，所以不用吼，鵰就聽得見）*可是，這有什麼好奇怪的？我們的總人口數就是你們的四倍！

但你們在數學、物理、化學、生化、工程與電腦等高科技領域等畢業生人數，是我們的十倍以上。這我沒說錯了吧？我第一次就應該沒聽錯吧？

With that the Dragon took flight with the Eagle flying in close formation as they soared from the highly developed coastal cities to the less developed industrial and farming regions in central and western Dragonland. The Eagle was struck by the contrasts of ancient mixed with modern; of the thriving cities and factories in close proximity to antiquated burrows, time-worn tenaments and lean-tos; of the most modern highways stretching from north to south, and east to west, rivaling any in the West, not far from dusty, rut-filled dirt roads and streets in the smaller cities; with most of the farming done on small plots of land, tilled and harvested mostly by hand tools; with space-age technology side by side with bronze-age ecology. But mostly with the teeming masses of trucks, buses, trains, bicycles, cars, push-carts and millions upon millions of pedestrians all with the same goal—to work and earn a seat at the banquet table of TwentyFirst Century progress.

*(catching its breath)* Slow down, Dragon. You don't have to flap your wings like I do. I have been counting the number of universities that we have been flying over. You have more in Beijing than we have in most of our states! You mentioned in one of our early discussions that you have four times the number of graduating students from your universities than we have from ours.

*(flying closer so the Eagle could hear without having to shout)* But why should that not be expected? We have four times your population!

Yet you have more than ten times the number of university graduates in the high tech majors such as math, physics, chemistry, bioscience, engineering and computer technology. That's true, isn't it? I heard you right the first time?

以前，遍佈全世界的先進產品與服務，都是由你們發明、製造和營銷的，全球經濟都在你們的掌握之中。那些知識，遠方的我們可不是沒注意。我們現在也製造並促銷同樣的產品和服務。我們未來的成就，取決於我們能否運用尖端科技發明並製造產品和服務。掌握這些技術，能夠提升我們的競爭力。

西方得醒醒了！我們從幼兒到高三的教育頂多算中等品質，在您剛提到的科目裡，我們學生的成績也在全球墊底。我們已經失去製造優勢，我擔心科技優勢也差不多了。我們的孩子，很快就會開始把弄龍族發明的小玩意兒了！科學展在年輕學生的心中更沒什麼地位了。

看看下面那一大群學生。請注意，他們不是在運動。那是成千上萬的年輕學生在參加各地的科學展比賽。他們就像運動明星一樣，亟欲拿出好成績。別以為我在炫耀。雖然我們的學生通常每天上學做功課的時間約十小時，還得學英文，但他們該學的還很多。一方面，他們在學校沒什麼紀律問題，不但尊敬老師，且幾乎每個都積極進取，想拿好成績。另一方面，在批判性思考、創新表達與創業精神等項目上，他們也試著迎頭趕上。

In the past, you invented, manufactured and marketed advanced products and services worldwide to dominate the global economy. That knowledge did not go unnoticed by those of us in faraway lands. We now manufacture and market those same goods and services. Our future success will depend on our ability to invent and create products and services using leading edge technologies. Mastering technology will give us the competitive edge.

We need a wake-up call in the West! Our kindergarten through 12th grade education is mediocre at best, and our students are among the lowest scoring in the world in the subjects you are talking about. We've already lost the manufacturing edge and I fear we have lost the technological edge as well. Our kids will soon be fiddling on gadgets from Dragonland! Science fairs are not status symbols among our young students.

Look at that large congregation of students down there. Notice that they aren't playing a sport. We have many thousands of young students competing in science fairs throughout our land. They are as eager to do well as if they were star athletes. But I don't want to appear boastful. While it's true that our students normally go to classes and do their homework approximately ten hours every weekday, and are required to study English, they have much to learn. On the one hand, they have few discipline problems at school, they respect their teachers and virtually all of them are ambitious and diligent about doing well in their classes. On the other hand, they are trying to catch up in the areas of critical thinking, creative self-expression and individual entrepreneurship.

我們雙方都需要更多交換學生！我們的自我表達與果斷，再加上你們的自律、毅力和團隊精神，可能形成強大的綜合效應。

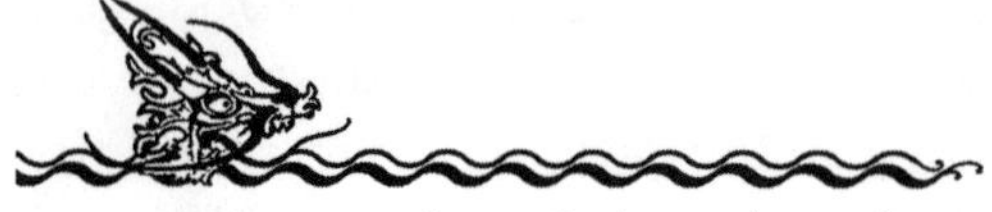

已經形成了。我們許多頂尖的學生，曾在你們最頂尖的大學讀過書，並把這些經驗帶回家。希望同樣的現象，會發生在你們在我國的留學生身上。主辦奧運會和世博會，讓大家對龍地上發生的質變很感興趣。

我也記得不久以前吧，學校裡學的知識就夠用了，足以讓你靠它過一輩子。隨著知識的急速擴張，學校學的不夠了。每天都有數百篇科學類論文發表。每隔卅秒，某個技術團隊就會推出一項新發明。

我再同意不過了。我認為學校教育的效用，大概只能維持十八個月，甚至加上碩士或博士學位也一樣。過去員工會指望老闆提供終生的工作保障。這已經不可能了，因為發展中國家正步步進逼。員工應該期望的，是由雇主提供技能訓練與終生學習的機會，因為沒人能提供一輩子的就業保障了。

這個發展我們到現在都難以接受。老闆沒辦法提供長期的工作保

We both need more exchange students! Our individual self-expression and assertiveness, combined with your self-discipline, resilience and team play could have some powerful synergy.

It already has. Many of our top students have studied at your best universities and are bringing those experiences home. Hopefully, the same will happen with your students who spend time with us. Hosting an Olympiad and World Trade Fair has brought more attention to the metamorphosis taking place throughout our land.

I also remember that it wasn't all that long ago when what you learned in school was largely all you needed to learn; you could rely on that knowledge for the rest of your life. With knowledge expanding exponentially, this is no longer true. Hundreds of scientific papers are published daily. Every thirty seconds, some new technology team produces yet another innovation.

I couldn't agree more. I believe the shelf-life of formal education is about eighteen months, even if it comes with a masters or doctoral degree. There was a time when workers expected an employer to guaranty them lifetime job security. That is no longer possible because of competition coming from developing nations. What workers should expect is gaining employability skills and lifelong learning from employers, since no one can guaranty lifelong employment.

That's been a hard pill for us to swallow. Workers dedicate themselves to an employer who can no longer offer them secu-

障，員工卻還要全心投入。西方社會因此出現巨大動盪，並可能導致隔離主義與保護主義，以減緩來自海外的競爭。可是，這種思維是個陷阱，對不對？

是的。在我們快速工業化與發展的同時，這將會是嚴峻的挑戰。我曾說過，我們是個以家立國的民族，一定會考慮決策對民眾的衝擊。要在「貧」與「富」之間取得均衡很不容易。咱們飛到目前為止，您應該已經發現主要港口附近的沿岸城市，正在享受辛勤工作換取的果實，且速度超過中部省分的居民，但中部各省，正是我國國民最集中的區域。

這難題怎麼解決？

工作努力，產能就增加。產能一增加，物品、營收和利潤就增加。利潤一增加，我們就能蓋設備更精良的新工廠，創造更多就業機會。為容納這麼多勞工，我們每卅天，就必須建造一個相當於貴國費城般規模的城市。

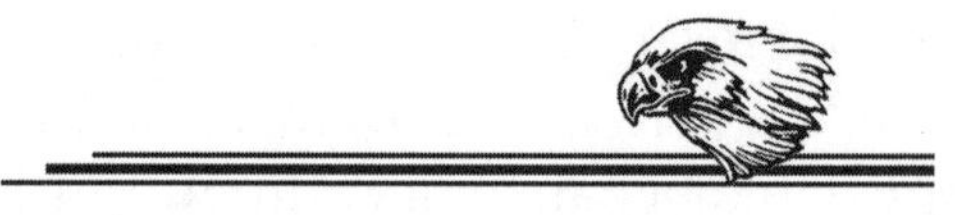

您在開玩笑吧？

絕不。看看下面那些數以萬計用來蓋高樓的巨型起重機。這些機具和來自全球的混凝土，大多不過在這幾年間，就運到廣州、福州、杭州、上海和北京。

rity for the long-term. This is causing great unrest in our part of the world and can lead to isolationism and protectionism as a buffer against competition abroad. But that kind of thinking is a trap, isn't it?

Yes, it is. And it will be a major challenge for us as we industrialize and prosper on a fast track. I have told you before, we are a nation of families and are always concerned about the impact of our decisions on our citizens. It will not be easy for us to balance our "haves" with our "have-nots." As you have seen during our brief flight, our coastal communities near our major ports are experiencing the harvests of their hard work much more rapidly than those living in the central provinces. And the majority of our population resides in the center of our country.

So how do you deal with this dilemma?

By working hard, we increase productivity. By increasing productivity, we produce more goods, revenues and profits. With more profits we expand into newer, better-equipped factories and create more jobs. To house more workers, we need to create a city the size of your Philadelphia about every 30 days.

You're serious?

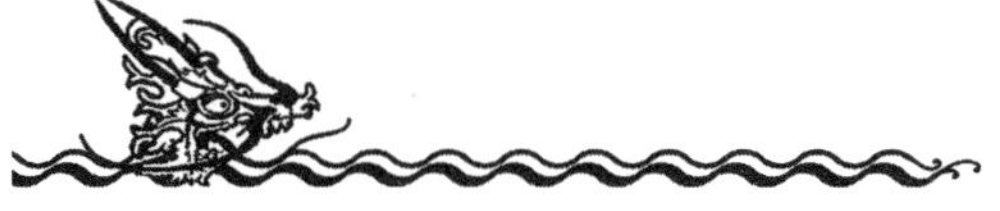

Of course, I am. Look down at the thousands of giant cranes used to erect high-rises. Most of them and most of the world's cement have been shipped to Guangzhou, Fuzhou, Hangzhou, Shanghai and Beijing during just the past few years.

*（緊盯著下面的景象）*我好像在看科幻電影，一大群機械人正聚集起來征服世界。

最大的挑戰，在於持續拉高國內生產毛額，並提升勞動與管理水準，讓他們做好進軍國際貿易的準備，同時又不能造成經濟過熱，以免導致貨幣供需不穩定。我們正在放寬政策限制，讓國外的投資、銀行和金融服務業者在本地開業。

飛越繁榮且美麗的杭州後，鵰跟著龍沿東岸向北前進。鵰驚訝地發現似乎有好幾群城市集中在一起，沿著水岸邊發展，其建築美得讓鵰忘了呼吸，與他以前看過的大都會不一樣。

龍兄，我們在這兒盤旋一下。眼前所見簡直難以置信。那些集中的城市群究竟是什麼？看起來好像三、四個全新的紐約曼哈頓連在一起。

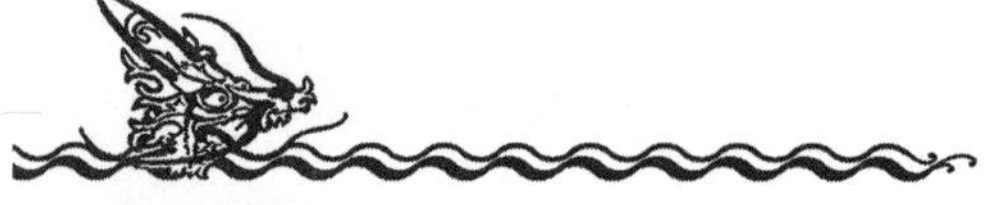

那是一個城，鵰兄！是上海。

我到現在都不相信今天的老上海，已說得上是全世界最蓬勃精彩的城市，其中有些象徵傳統龍族的有趣建築，以及許多我們眼中實體的未來世界。

壯觀！我知道你們的汽油消耗量，僅次於我國。從成長率來看，你們未來的汽車數量和汽油消耗量，將超過所有西方國家的總和。別

*(fixing its vision on the spectacle below)* It reminds me of a science fiction movie, with giant robots assembled to conquer the world.

The most difficult challenge is to keep growing our GNP, increase the skill level of our workers and their managers, to prepare them for global commerce, and to do all this without over-heating our economy which could cause instability in our monetary supply and demand. We are liberalizing our policies toward foreign investment and foreign banking and financial services operating in our land.

Flying with the Dragon north along the East coast from the thriving, beautiful city of Hangzhou, the Eagle was enthralled with what appeared to be a group of cities in one cluster all along the water front. The architecture was breathtaking, unlike any major metropolises it had ever encountered.

Let's circle here for a while, Dragon. I can't believe what I'm seeing. What are those incredible cities over there, all bunched together? They look like three or four, glistening, new Manhattans in New York next to one another.

That is one city, Eagle! That is Shanghai. It's still hard for me to believe that old Shanghai today is arguably the most vibrant, exciting city in the world, with some of the most interesting architecture representing ancient Dragonland and our own version of many real-life Epcot Centers.

Spectacular! I understand that you are only second to us in your use of gasoline. At your rate of growth, you will have more automobiles and use more gas than all of our Western countries

忘了空氣污染這東西！我們有九個城市人口數超過一百萬。我從剛才數到現在，下面就已經有超過卄個這樣的城市。

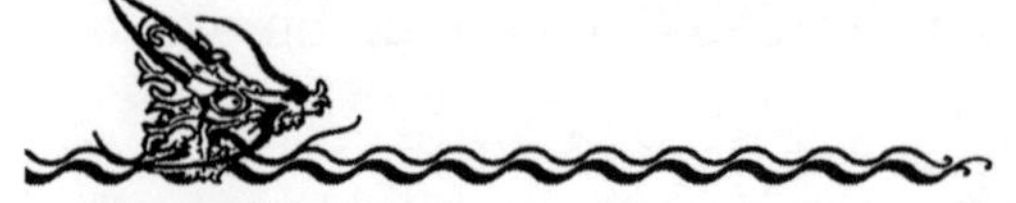

*（搖著巨大的頭）*居民超過一百萬的城市，遠超過一百個。我們堵車的時候，您絕對沒看過，「尖峰時間」一塞就是好幾個小時。唉，進步的代價。有時我會想念簡單點的生活，像是騰空飛翔、徒步行走等等。（對我來說，徒步要同時用好多條腿。）

難怪你們要用這麼多起重機和混凝土！你們基本上每個月，就要蓋一座居民遠超過二百萬的城市。真是不可思議！

因此您得多待些時間親眼看看。別忘了到我們在杭州、上海和北京的高檔餐廳吃個飯，絕對不輸紐約、芝加哥、巴黎和倫敦。

很糟糕的，是我們的飲食習慣，正因為貴國的飲食文化而墮落。我們在過去五年開的速食連鎖店數目，幾乎跟你們過去四十年開的一樣多。

*（邊盤旋邊朝下望）*看看那些麥當勞、必勝客和肯德基。怎麼會這樣！幾乎每一家都那麼大，至少二層樓高。大多數是得來速嗎？

combined. And don't forget about smog! We have nine cities with populations of a million or more. So far, I've counted over twenty with more people than that.

*(shaking its giant head)* We have well over one hundred cities with more than a million people each. We already have traffic jams like you have never seen, and our "rush hour" lasts for several hours. Ah, the price of progress. Sometimes I pine for the simpler life of winged flight and walking on foot. (In my case, I should say many, many feet.)

No wonder you are hoarding all the building cranes and cement! You are building a city of well over two million inhabitants almost every month. That's hard to fathom!

That's why you need to extend your visits to see for yourself. But be sure to dine at our upscale restaurants in Hangzhou, Shanghai and Beijing, which rival those in New York, Chicago, Paris and London.

Unfortunately, we also have been seduced by your culture in terms of our eating habits. We have opened almost as many fast-food franchises during the past five years as you did in the past forty years.

*(circling and peering down)* Look at all the Golden Arches,™ Pizza Hut™s and KFC™s. Unbelievable! And most of them are gigantic with more than one floor. Are most of them drive-thrus?

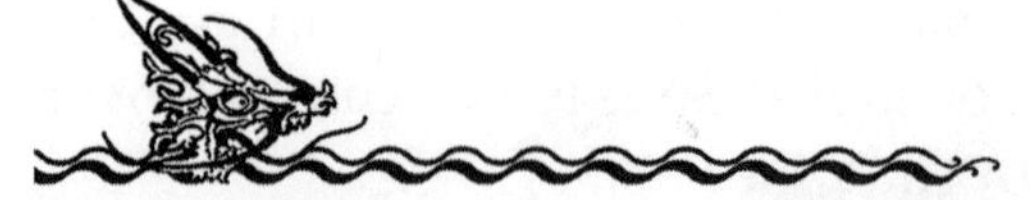

不是，大多數是內用！您這輩子絕對沒看過這麼多的漢堡、薯條、炸雞和比薩。我之前說過，吃是我們最偉大的社交娛樂和禮儀之一。得來速才正開始普及。真不敢想像車隊會排得多長！不久後我們大概就不能叫它們速食餐廳了。叫停車場大概還比較合適！

恕我冒犯，如果你們繼續模仿我們的生活方式，體型過大的龍就要出現了。我們的孩子吃得比玩得還凶，超重造成的副作用，絕不是多些肉而已。

這就是貴我兩國雙方的父母，都更須要為下一代以身作則。父母親不是不懂，但聽廣告的話來做輕鬆多了。生活會跟著流行走。之前，我們不也一致認為今天的父母給孩子錢，卻不給孩子*時間*。

而且孩子們只會模仿同伴，並按照著成年榜樣所教的去做。觀察、模仿和重複，最後內化成反射習慣。不論正面或負面的生活方式，都會養成習慣。近朱者赤，近墨者黑。

沒錯，有樣就學樣。這就是為什麼學習是一輩子的事，而不是蒐集事實和技能就行了。這也表示正式的學校教育並不夠。在現代世界

No, most of them are eat-ins! You've never seen so many burgers, fries, chicken and pizza in your life. I told you before that eating is one of our great social pastimes and ceremonies. The drive-thrus are just starting to proliferate. Imagine how long those lines will be! It may be a misnomer to refer to them as fast-food restaurants in the near future. They may become parking lots!

If you'll pardon my insolence, you are going to have some oversized Dragons, if you follow our lifestyle. Our kids go out to eat more than they go out to play, and being overweight carries more side effects than simply extra baggage.

That's why your parents and our parents must become better role models and leaders for the next generation. They all know better, but give in because it's easier to go along with what's advertised. Life imitates fashion. As we agreed earlier, we spend *money on* instead of *time with* our children.

And they only imitate what their peers are doing, and what adult role models teach them. Observation, imitation, and repetition become internalized as reflex habits. Winning and losing lifestyles are both habit-forming. We become that to which we are most exposed.

Yes, we do become that to which we are most exposed. That's why the acquisition of knowledge is a lifelong experience, not a collection of facts or skills. It also means much more than formal classroom knowledge. In a world in which working and socializ-

裡，合作與交際是如此重要，意味著學習能讓你更深入瞭解自己與同伴，其中包含哪些行為及選擇是對是錯。

說得好，況且我們這兒有個好消息，那就是我們終於能從健康與人際關係的角度看這件事情。您也知道抽煙在西方已經不流行了，所以煙草公司都願意砸大錢打廣告，鼓勵開發中國家的民眾繼續抽煙。

我同意在戒煙這方面，我們應該向您學習。咱們打個商量：你們每繳出一把手槍，我們就交一條香菸到資源回收中心。

龍兄，等等，您又在找我麻煩了。沒必要打「暴力社會」這張牌。我認為在如何成為「慈善社會」這方面，你們該學的還很多。好*「風水」*的概念，也該應用在貴國的城市環境上。許多我們飛過的城市，空氣污染都和洛杉磯一樣嚴重。

由於工業化快速，我們也曾必須在事後把巢清理乾淨，而且要做的還很多。成長越快，維持城市生態的健康就越是個挑戰。

我知道我們的快速成長是兩面刃，但我還是忍不住要善意地稍稍損您一下。您剛才已經慢慢開始說教了。

ing with people is essential, it also means deepening your understanding of yourself and others; including healthy and unhealthy behaviors and choices.

Amen, and a patch of good news from our culture is that we are finally recognizing this in terms of our health and personal relationships. You already know that smoking is no longer in fashion in the West, which is why all the big advertising dollars by tobacco companies are being spent to promote the habit in the developing countries.

I agree that we should follow your lead when it comes to kicking the smoking habit. Let's make a deal. We'll turn in a carton of cigarettes to a recycling center, for every hand-gun that you turn in.

Now, now, Dragon, you're ruffling my feathers again. No need to play the "violent society" card. From my perch, you've got lessons of your own to learn about becoming a "benevolent society," and you need to apply good *"feng shui"* to the environment in your cities. Many of the cities we've flown over have been as smoggy as Los Angeles.

As a result of our own rapid industrialization, we have had to clean up our nest after the fact. And we have a long, long way to go. The faster you grow, the greater your own challenges will be to maintain healthy ecology in your cities.

I am aware that our rapid growth is a two-edged sword, but I couldn't resist a friendly, little jab. You were beginning to sermonize a bit.

我只是想提醒您，生活方式與生活品質之間的因果關係，西方終於開始瞭解了。

龍點頭示意，然後加速飛越更多的城市與梯田。從天安門廣場、紫禁城、北京奧運中心體育場到長城，鵬都讚嘆不已，還不斷飛高，試著從只有鵬能享有的各個角度，欣賞這壯觀的景色。鵬相信即使在外太空軌道繞行的航天飛機，都仍然能夠清晰地辨識出這些景象。

在世界聞名的西安兵馬俑，龍特別安排了個別導覽，而八千多座沈寂了二千年才出土的仿真軍人及戰鬥馬車，尤其讓鵬感到敬畏不已。

我們為什麼不待久一點？我從沒看過這麼神奇的東西！當初一定動用了成千上萬的工匠，花了數十年的時間，才創造出如此寶藏。

我們可以下次再來。今天博物館不對外開放，所以我們才能造訪，同時不驚動成千上萬前來參觀如此重大考古發現的訪客。此外，我把壓軸好戲留在最後，得在太陽下山前趕到西南方才行。

話一說完，龍升空朝西急飛，鵬緊追在後。鵬發現更多來自北方與東方沿岸的高速公路與鐵路，綿延不絕地向南方與西方延伸。鵬提醒龍這一點的時候，龍微微一笑，表示很快地，將有條陸路從上海直達歐洲，子彈列車在各主要城市間行駛。畢竟，正如龍先前所

**All I was trying to say is that we in the West finally are beginning to understand the cause and effect relationship between lifestyle choices and our quality of life.**

The Dragon nodded and picked up speed flying over still more cities and terraced farmland. From Tiananmen Square, the Forbidden City and the Olympic Stadium in Beijing, to the Great Wall—which so impressed the Eagle that it flew as high as it could to take in the spectacle as only an Eagle could, marveling that it no doubt could be clearly distinguished in its entirety from a space shuttle orbiting in outer space.

The Eagle was especially awed by the private tour the Dragon had arranged of the world-famous Terra Cotta Warriors and Horses in Xian, with more than 8,000 life-size figures of soldiers and horse-drawn chariots uncovered and preserved after 2,000 years.

**Why can't we stay longer? I've never seen anything so amazing! It must have taken thousands of craftsmen and several decades to create such treasures.**

We can come back another time. Today, the site is closed to the public, which is why we were able to stop without creating chaos among the thousands of visitors that come to view this most significant archeological discovery. Besides, I have saved my final surprise for you for the last and we must hurry to the southwest before the sun goes down.

With that, the Dragon rose in the sky and rapidly headed to the west, with the Eagle in close pursuit. The Eagle noticed more superhighways and railroad tracks stretching from the far north, and from the coastlines in the east, to the farthest reaches of the south and west. When it mentioned this to the Dragon, the Dragon smiled and acknowledged that soon there would be an overland route from Shanghai all the way to Europe and bullet trains between major internal cities. After all, the Dragon had offered, there

說，本地流動的龍民，數目高於世界各地。

接近湖北宜昌的時候，鵬看見一座混凝土建築，其巨大難以理解。

這真是在開我玩笑！！一定是夕陽把我的視力都弄糊了。我沒看錯吧？是水壩嗎？

沒錯，您沒看錯。那是三峽大壩。

這簡直讓我們的胡佛水壩看起來像蓄水池！！老天，簡直跟我們在舊金山的金門大橋一樣長，高度至少在二倍以上。我得靠近點看，確定我不須要戴隱形眼鏡。

大壩的功能在於調節長江的洪水，同時提供本地一百八十億瓦的電力。

*（從壩頂下降至底下的江面）*這鐵定至少有六百英尺高，我還看見五個調節江面高度用的船閘。

船要通過所有五道船閘，得花約三個小時，然後才能繼續航程。除了防洪與發電外，大壩使長江乾淨多了，也不會大幅衝擊周遭的環境。

are more people on the move than anywhere else in the world.

As they approached Yichang City in Hubei Province, the Eagle saw a concrete structure so massive that it defied logic.

You've got to be putting me on! It must be the late afternoon sun that is blurring my vision. Is that what I think it is? A dam?

No, your eyes are not deceiving you. That is Three Gorges Dam.

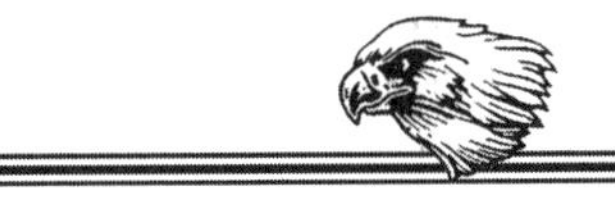

It makes our Hoover Dam look like a reservoir! Why that's got to be as wide as our Golden Gate Bridge in San Francisco, yet at least twice as tall. I need a closer look to make sure I don't need contact lenses.

Its main purpose is to control the flood waters of the Yangtze River, and, at the same time, provide the region with 18 gigawatts of electrical power.

*(soaring from the top of the dam to the river below)* It's got to be at least 600 feet high, and I counted five different ship locks to handle the elevations.

It takes about three hours for boats to pass through all five locks and continue on their voyages. In addition to flood control and the benefits of electrical power that will be generated, the river will be much cleaner without too great an impact on the surrounding ecology.

你們遷移了多少居民？

因為江面升高，超過一百萬居民必須遷移，是人類史上最大規模的遷移計畫。幸好十二個新城鎮所提供的現代化住宅，民眾都挺滿意的。跟上，該回去了。太陽下山後天很快就黑了

他們回到龍穴時，清風徐徐，空氣中帶著涼意。龍再泡了一壺綠茶，然後與鵬談論今天的所見所聞，為一天的交流做個總結。

天啊，這熱茶來得正好。我以為我的翅膀要凍僵，回不來了。

看了這麼多，感覺如何？

如此人力資源運用上的奇蹟，真是前所未見。謝謝您這趟精彩充實的導覽。我在一天之內，瞭解大家都該天天學的重要性，不論是工作或生活，都絕不要自以為什麼都懂了。

How big a population did you have to displace?

Due to higher water levels created, over a million people have had to be resettled. It is the largest resettlement project ever undertaken in the world. The good news is that the people are enjoying more modern housing provided for them in 12 new cities. Come, we must go back now. The sun has set and soon it will be dark.

When they arrived back at the Dragon's cave, there was a brisk wind blowing, with a chill in the air. After making a fresh pot of green tea, the Dragon and Eagle finished their conversation about what they had seen and discussed.

Boy, this hot tea is just what I needed. I thought my wings were going to ice up before we made it back.

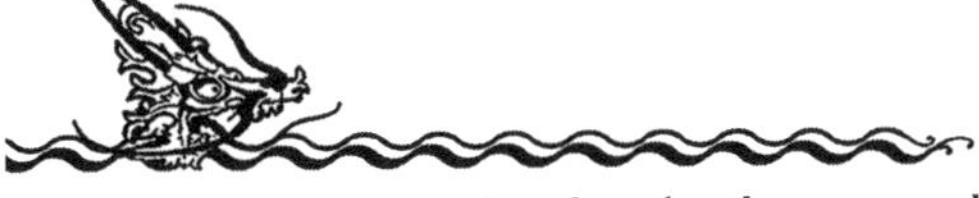

So what do you think of what you have seen?

I've never witnessed such a miracle in the use of human resources. Thanks for an exciting and rewarding tour. In a single day, I have come to understand how important it is for all of us to learn something new every day and never take for granted that we know enough to be complacent in our professional and personal lives.

不論是我們的歷史、我們的錯誤還是你們的錯誤，希望都有值得學習之處。許多隨著生活水準提高而開始浮現的問題，你們當初怎麼解決，我們現在又怎麼面對，也值得雙方學習。若我們覺得邊嘗試邊修正學得比較快，就非常糟糕了。千萬不要忘記生活水準，指的是有多少錢可以花，而生活品質，指的是時間運用得多好。

並在同時享有更多的健康和喜樂。

當然，為了不讓您覺得我今天又有說教的嫌疑，小的在此稟報：不論我的年紀多大，我都視自己為「永遠的學生」，而不是什麼專家。

什麼？我的朋友裡就屬您最有智慧。

自認為專家有其危險性，特別是對事物不再好奇。你不再像孩子般受到好奇心驅使，而只想捍衛自己之前擁抱、相信或發展的理念。你只敢給保證無誤的答案，而不願以「不知道」來解放自己。終生學習的領袖，絕不會忘記要學的還很多。知識與經驗可能使他們成為導師，但他們卻永遠視自己為學生。

Hopefully, we can learn from our history, our mistakes, your mistakes; as well as from your solutions and our own approaches to many of the problems that we are just beginning to face as our standard of living increases. It would be unfortunate indeed, if we felt that trial and error were better teachers. We must never forget that standard of living is how much money we have to spend, and that quality of life is how well we spend our time.

And having more health and joy in the process.

Of course, and lest you think I've been, as you say, sermonizing somewhat myself today, may I humbly say that I consider myself, regardless of my age, as a "permanent student," rather than an expert.

What do you mean? You're the wisest person I've ever encountered.

There are dangers in thinking of yourself as an expert—especially the danger of losing your sense of wonder. Instead of being driven by curiosity, like a child, you become driven to defend what you've previously embraced, believed or developed. Reciting safe answers now, you stop saying the liberating words, "I don't know." Leaders who continue learning throughout their lives never forget they always have more to learn. Although their knowledge and experience may have made them teachers, they continue to think of themselves as students.

所以我們要不斷精進，但避免自以為是。

完全正確。鵰兄，若您不介意，今天我覺得比平常還累些。我們匆匆飛了這麼遠，所以我想獨自打坐，回想今天的交流。請別以為我在下逐客令。今天真的充滿啟示與靈性。

然後，巨龍就拖著疲累的身軀返回龍穴，告訴自己下次一定要養足精神。就在鵰準備升空時，龍回頭說了最後一句話。

避免自以為是的最主要原因，莫過於即使我們不斷精進，成見仍可能蒙蔽我們發掘並孕育新靈感的能力。鵰兄，我們的偉大成就，來自於過去許多寶貴的教訓，雖然我必會珍惜，並熱切地想與您分享，但我真的也很想體會並沈浸在追尋新靈感的驚喜中。

我要成為不忘本的未來學家，但非只會挖掘過去的考古學家。明天見。

So we must continue to gain expertise, but avoid thinking like an expert.

Exactly. And now, if you'll excuse me, Eagle, I find myself a bit more weary than usual. That was a long flight in such a short period, so I think I will take my leave to meditate and ponder on what we have exchanged. Don't mistake my decision to cut this meeting short today. It was enlightening and soulful.

With that, the huge Dragon lumbered back into its lair, promising to be more invigorating next time. And just as the Eagle was about to take flight, the Dragon turned and made a final comment.

The most compelling reason to avoid thinking like an expert, even while continuing to acquire expertise, is that our assumptions may cloud our ability to generate and work with new ideas. And, Eagle, as passionate as I am about hanging on to the invaluable lessons from the past that made us great and share them with you, I do so want to savor and revel in the thrill and promise of fresh, new ideas.

I want to be a futurist, while maintaining my cultural roots; not an archeologist, digging in the past. See you tomorrow.

# 摘要

第六回

# Summary

CHAPTER 6

## 心智王國

## Empires of the Mind

# 龍親口告訴我們…
# Straight from the Dragon's mouth...

☯ 老子是我們最推崇的哲學家之一。龍地上的龍，會永遠推崇他的話，尤其是：「*知人者智，知己者明*」以及「***悠兮其貴言。功成事遂，百姓皆謂：『我自然。』***」

從古到今，這個忠告對東西方而言，都不像今天這般如此重要。

☯ 我們擁有的技術能力，理應能讓我們做更多的好事，但卻遭誤用在許多邪惡的事上。若今天有什麼課教的是「***智者生存***」，而非「適者生存」，我一定馬上報名。

☯ The Dragons in my realm will forever revere the words of one of our greatest philosophers Lao Tzu... especially: ***To know others is intelligence; to know myself is wisdom.*** And: ***A leader is best when people barely knows he exists. When his work is done, his aim fulfilled, they will say: "We did it ourselves."***

Never before in our ancient history has this advice been more critical for the East or West.

☯ We now possess the technology to do so much good in our world, but it continues to be used for evil in too many places. Sign me up for the class that reminds us it's no longer the survival of the fittest, but ***the survival of the wisest.***

# 鵰的看法則是…

# From the Eagle's point of view...

✱ 鵰族的老鵰眾多，但都不比老子還老。然而，我們最傑出的盟友之一邱吉爾說得好：*未來的王國將是心智的王國*。的確，知識就是力量，而這股力量將中止軍備競賽，讓我們能空出雙手擁抱美善。因此，我們應共同努力建立互信，而非敵意與仇恨。

✱ We have many old Eagles in Eagleland, but none as old as Lao Tzu. However, Winston Churchill, one of our most brilliant allies ever, was also correct when he said that *the empires of the future will be empires of the mind.* It's true: knowledge is power—power that leaves the arms race in the dust and frees our arms to embrace that which is good. So let's work mutually on what builds trust, not on what produces rancor and hate.

# 龍親口告訴我們…
# Straight from the Dragon's mouth...

☯ 您到東方來的時候，要做好多喝茶的準備，而且還得喝很多。如此美味的飲料，我們已經享用數千年了，而且茶飲營造的氣氛，最能激發熱烈的討論。我想一開始，慢慢喝茶對鵰而言頗為困難。然而，過去幾個月，我發現我的朋友步調放慢了，想得也比較深了。誰說老鳥學不了新招的啊？

☯ When you come to the East, be prepared to drink tea. Lots of tea. We've indulged in this fine drink for millennia, and we've found it to be the perfect liquid formula to help create an environment for lively discussion. I think it was hard for Eagle at first to sip its tea slowly. But over these past few months I've seen my friend slow down and become more contemplative. Who ever said that you can't teach an old bird new tricks?

## 鵬的看法則是…

## *From the Eagle's point of view...*

✯ 幸好幾個月前我遇見龍，否則我這如羽毛般平順的一生，就可能過得空虛貧乏。一開始，我只想跟這位多腳的朋友鬥嘴，但後來卻只想靜下來。我現在很慶幸當初決定以最佳的身心狀況與龍交流。希望我倆間單純的密切交流，能擴及至成千上萬的龍與鵬，讓他們永世得以彼此對話、爭論、辯論與學習。

✯ I have a feeling my fine-feathered life would never have been fulfilling had I not met Dragon a few months ago. At first, I wanted to argue with my many-footed friend; then I had a desire to be silent. Now I'm glad I choose to engage Dragon with all the strength of my body and the best of my mind. It's my hope that our simple *tête-à-tête* will expand to include thousands of Eagles and Dragons who will talk, argue, debate and learn from each other for eons to come.

# 龍親口告訴我們…
# Straight from the Dragon's mouth...

☯ 我說正規教育的功效平均只能維持約十八個月時，是很正經的。碩士和博士學位也一樣。因為龍瞭解這一點，所以會持續地研究、學習、發明、應變且拼命工作。

☯ 沒錯，我們想成為全球的技術領先者，而且時日已近。然而，我們也希望與其它工業國家保持良好關係。若鵰想照著我們的規模競爭，就得加緊腳步。終究，中國每卅天就建造一個如費城般大小的城市，是美國可能無法比擬的。與其試著跟我們競爭，咱們還不如共同完成這些驚人的目標，為大家創造雙贏。

☯ I'm serious when I say the average shelf-life of formal education is approximately 18 months—masters and doctoral degrees notwithstanding. Because our Dragons know this, we will continue to study, learn, invent, improvise and work by the sweat of our brows.

☯ Yes, we want to be the world's technological leader—and we soon will be. But we also want to have an amicable relationship with the rest of the industrial world. But the Eagles must play catch up if they want to compete on our scale. In the end, Eagles may never be able to compete with a country that builds a city the size of Philadelphia every 30 days. But instead of trying to compete with us, let's do these amazing things together so that it's a win-win situation for all.

## 鵰的看法則是…

# From the Eagle's point of view...

✵ 對我而言，其中一次為時較久的茶會尤其難以忘懷。那天，我痛苦地意識到未來的領袖，不一定再是西方。其實，我們說不定早已是虛位領袖，以為自己還在引領方向。要鵰族意會甚至承認這一點，是非常困難的，但我們若不學習新的語言，不多聽少說，不從嶄新的觀點看待商務，並承認自己不是「萬事通」，我們的創意泉源就即將乾涸了。

因此，我跟龍一樣十分贊成舉辦更多的茶會，但不一定要在洞裡，如此方能好好坐下反省輝煌的過去，但同時匯集彼此的專長，以創造更光明美好的未來。

✵ One of those long tea sessions with Dragon was particularly memorable to me. It was when I was painfully reminded that the West is no longer necessarily in the driver's seat. In fact, we may already have become backseat drivers, thinking our hands are still on the wheel. It's difficult for Eagles to fathom—or even admit it—but if we do not learn new languages, listen more than talk, look at business with fresh, new eyes, and admit that *we do not know it all*, then our creative days will indeed be numbered.

So, like Dragon, I'm all for more tea parties—not necessarily in caves, however—where we can sit and reflect on our glorious pasts while we marshal our mutual skills for a better, brighter future.

# 龍親口告訴我們…

# *Straight from the Dragon's mouth...*

☯ 未來，希望有更多鵰來體驗這個古老與未來兼容的國家。唯有親身體驗，方能瞭解彼此的難處、文化與機會。

☯ Hopefully, more Eagles will visit our land to experience antiquity, alongside the world of tomorrow. Only by first-hand experience will we be able to appreciate each others' struggles, cultures and opportunities.

## 鵰的看法則是…

# *From the Eagle's point of view...*

✶ 幾個月前，我好想跟龍比個高下，更不想祝龍一切順利。今天則不同了。這就是我為什麼不希望龍吃太多速食…用香菸提早自殺，或者呼吸骯髒的空氣，也就是工業進步下的致命惡果。西方終於開始有能力解決這些切身的環保問題。今天，我想盡一己之力協祝龍把這個訊息分享給龍族。這個充斥著污染的世界，該清一清了，而且我們可以一次從一條龍、一隻鵰開始。龍兄，別懷疑，老鳥*還是可以學新把戲的*。然而，做個有愛心的朋友，並不是什麼「把戲」。唯有如此，才能在這個日益縮小的世界生存並繁榮。

✶ A few months ago I felt so competitive with Dragon, that I would not have wished it the best. Now, I feel different. That's why I don't want Dragons to over-eat fast food…or kill themselves prematurely with cigarettes, or breathe putrid air, which is the lethal downside of industrial progress. The West is finally making progress in these vital personal environmental issues. Now, I want to do my part to help Dragon share this message with its fellow Dragons. It's time to clean up our debris-infested world, and we can do it one Eagle, one Dragon at a time. And yes, Dragon, we old birds actually *can learn new tricks*. But becoming a caring friend is not a "trick." It's the only way to survive and thrive in our ever-shrinking world.

第七回

CHAPTER 7

# 面向未來

# Facing the Future

過去幾個月，龍與鵬每星期都花數小時分享彼此的觀察。對雙方而言，今天算是畢業典禮吧。這會是他們最後一次見面，因為雙方都覺得讓茶葉沈沈底，好消化並回想這些日子的切磋，似乎是比較好的安排。他們同意這幾回合的交流，只不過開啟了未來長久對話的大門而已。畢竟，他們都相信五千多年的歷史，不是三言兩語就可以道盡的。一切都必須慢慢品嚐珍惜。把過去的教訓，運用於無法預知或甚至難以想像的未來，顯然絕對比扮事後諸葛困難許多。不可或缺的，是耐心、堅持、無條件的聆聽、遠見與創意。智慧切勿輕忽，必須加以內化，並奉行不渝。

雄偉的鵬從西方接近，揮舞翅膀的節奏，比前幾次的造訪都緩慢。這是趟矛盾的飛行。一方面，鵬急欲慶賀這個象徵彼此友誼的里程碑；另一方面，鵬因為彼此的首度接觸即將劃下句點而感傷。

巨鳥在日落前一刻抵達龍穴。鵬回首來時路，只見太陽這個炙熱的巨大火球，正緩緩地消失在遠方的地平線下。由於視野一望無際，不受任何障礙、逆溫或低雲層的遮蔽，太陽好像放大了百倍，彷彿是世界上最大的熱氣球，緩緩地冷卻下降，與地球相接觸。鵬曾從位於高山頂峰的巢裡看過多少日落，但眼前壯麗的景象，仍美得讓他摒住氣息。

鵬兄，好個盛大出場。我再怎麼事前排演，也不會這麼精彩。效果好得連我都有點兒喘不過氣！

龍兄，落日似乎與這個特別的儀式非常契合，但我得承認我對您的長相已經習慣了。

Today marked a commencement ceremony, a kind of graduation, for Dragon and Eagle who had been sharing personal observations for several hours a week, during the past few months. This was to be their last exchange for a while, both reasoning that it would be good to let the tea leaves settle a bit and for both to digest and ponder on what they had discussed. They agreed that these rendezvous were just the beginning of a dialogue that would continue through the years and decades ahead. After all, they concurred, over 5,000 years of history can't be gulped in a few sessions. It must be sipped and savored over time. And, of course, applying lessons from the past—to a future that no one could have foreseen nor even imagined—would be even more daunting than simple hindsight. Patience, persistence, unconditional listening, foresight and innovation would be required. Wisdom can't be trivialized. It must be internalized and embraced over time.

As the majestic Eagle approached from the West, the cadence of its wings was slower than in previous journeys to the East. There was ambivalence in its flight. Eagerness to celebrate a milestone in their relationship, and sadness in the realization that this was the final chapter in this first book of conversations between Dragon and Eagle.

It was just before sunset when the mighty bird arrived at the Dragon's lair. Glancing back from where it came, the Eagle saw the most enormous, molten, melon ball of a sun slipping slowly down toward the distant horizon. Because there were no visual obstructions, inversions or low cloud layers of any kind, the sun appeared to be magnified a hundred times. It was as if it were the world's largest hot air balloon, softly settling as it cooled and touched the earth. The Eagle had witnessed many sunsets from its perch high on the mountain's peak, but this magnificent spectacle took its breath away.

Grand entrance, Eagle. I couldn't have choreographed your arrival better myself. It even took some of the steam out of my breath!

Sunset seems to be a fitting time for this special ceremony, Dragon. But I must confess that I've grown accustomed to your face.

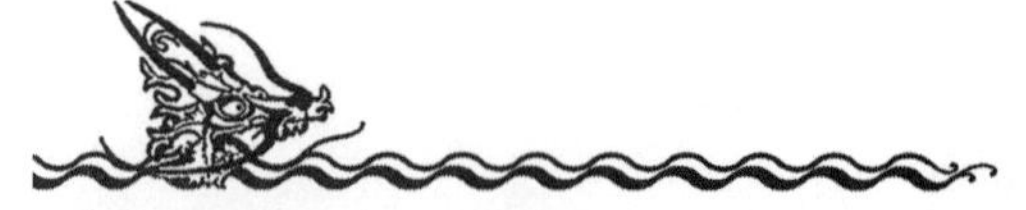

*（鼻子噴氣）*您別開始在我面前多愁善感起來。這不過是開場的結束而已。記住，大學畢業生認為「畢業典禮」象徵學業結束，但其實啊，他們才開始修「人生入門」哪，所以「畢業」應該改成「開業」才對。

我們見面的機會還很多。有件事現在談正好：下次我們挑日出見面，不知您意下如何？這樣您就能從不同的角度看日出。龍族相信我們即將步入前所未有的歷史新頁。

好，下次我們日出見，慶祝這段全新的友誼有個新的開始。

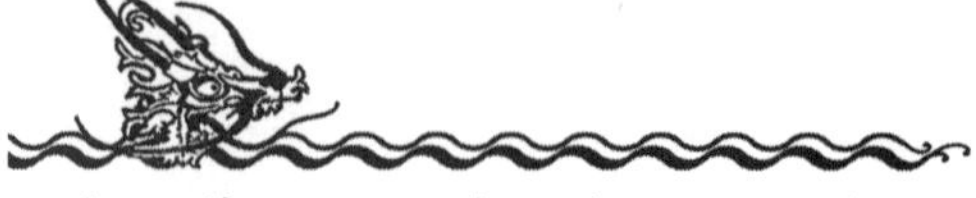

言歸正傳，小兄弟，我們到目前為止學了什麼，未來又該怎麼走？

我覺得最珍貴的教訓，就是我們必須相互學習彼此瞭解。我會謹記跟你們相比，西方社會是多麼少不更事，而我們又多麼須要勤發問、專心聽，並停止假設現在富強，就可因過去的功績而永遠富強。若我們志得意滿，鼻青臉腫則指日可待。

*(snorting)* Now don't go getting sentimental on me. This is simply the end of the beginning. Remember, although university graduates view the "commencement ceremony" to signify the finish of their studies, in all truth, they have only started Real World 101 Lessons, which is why the word "commence" means to begin, not to end.

We will have many tomorrows together. And, fittingly, let us agree that our next discussion will take place at sunrise. That way, you'll be able to see the sun from a different perspective. We Dragons believe that we are at the dawning of a new era in history, unlike any that has gone before.

Yes, we will meet at dawn next time to celebrate new beginnings in our relationship which is still in its infancy.

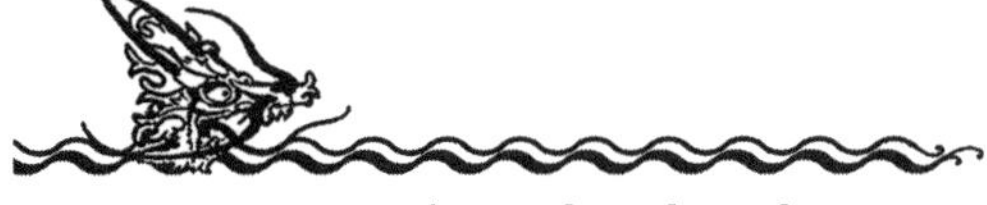

So, my young friend, what have we learned so far and where do we go from here?

For me, the most important lesson I've learned is how much we both need to learn from one another and about each other. I certainly will take home with me the realization of how young and inexperienced our Western society is, compared to yours, and how critical it is for us to ask more questions, listen intently, and abandon our assumptions that—because we have become rich and powerful—we will stay on top as if it were a status or permanent payoff for past achievements. If we rest on our laurels, we will tumble from our pedestals.

說得對。我覺得最有價值的，就是我的思路更敏銳，瞭解它國的文化，在創意、創新和自我表達上，有許多可取之處。此外，我們正從「壓抑致富」轉型為「鼓勵致富」，從等公家給轉型為自己闖，因此更要避免落入唯名利是圖的陷阱，誤以為名氣可以買到品格與內在價值。

那是西方普遍的誤解，我希望幼龍們能引以為戒。你們千萬不要變成一個「以貪婪、虛榮及物質為立國基礎，且只有我能享有自由與正義」的國家！我們這個種族多元國家，只要一個不小心，矢言效忠全民的誓詞就會變成「人不為己，天誅地滅」，而貴國以家立國的傳統，則可能被「有錢才是老大」的心態所取代。

而且，只要一不留心，咱們兩國都會重蹈覆轍走上沈淪之路。可是，我們不要把這次見面浪費在猜測未來上。咱們應該痛下決心乘風破浪，將末日預言一一粉碎。讓我們談談彼此成功的機會，忘記失敗的懲罰。

我今天想談的就是這些。我們必須為龍與鵰的新生代領袖預做準備。新一代的領袖，應說出大家該知道的，而不是大家想聽的。新一代的領袖，應告訴大家該怎麼做，而不該為選票輕諾寡信。新一

Well said. And, for me, my own awareness has been sharpened to understand that those outside our own culture have much to offer in the way of creativity, innovation and self-expression. At the same time, in our rush to move from "wealth discouragement" to "wealth encouragement" and from an entitlement society to an entrepreneurial society, we Dragons must avoid the pitfalls of worshiping lifestyles of the rich and famous, under the false belief that celebrity can purchase character and inner value.

That's a cultural misconception rampant in the West, which I hope your young Dragons don't fall prey to. What you don't want to create is "One nation, under greed, vain and visible, with liberty and justice for me!" If we're not careful, our pledge of allegiance to our nation, with all of its diverse citizens, will be replaced by "look out for number one" and your tradition of a nation of families, could be replaced with one where "he or she with the most toys wins."

And, if we're not careful, we both will repeat history all over again and follow that same precipitous path. But let's not waste this last meeting on premonitions. Instead, let's resolve to stem the tide and rise above all the doomsday predictions. Let us speak of mutual opportunities for success, rather than the penalties of failure.

That's what I came prepared for today. We need to set the stage for a new breed of leaders for all Eagles and Dragons. Leaders who will tell us what we need to know, not just tell us what we want to hear. Leaders who will tell us what we must do for ourselves, not make promises of what they will do for us if we vote

代的領袖，應該就目標提出清楚的建言，而不該含糊地重提古老的諺語。

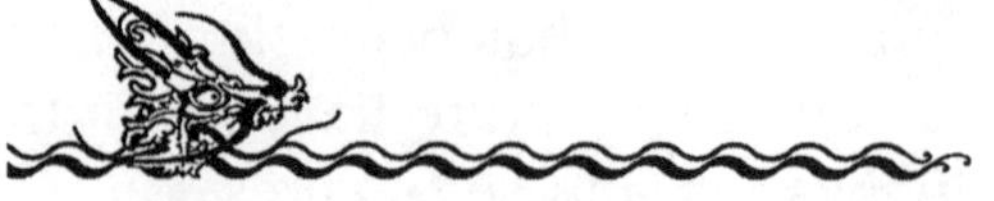

為什麼每次*古老*這個詞一出現，您就「斜眼」瞄我？

別怒氣沖沖嘛。我尊重您的年紀，以及多年累積的智慧，我也學到龍族非但不落後，進步的速度還遠超乎我們的想像。

少來這套。您到底想說什麼？

*（搖頭）*一扯到文化，根深蒂固的膝反射動作又來了。（您有膝蓋，對吧？）

我只是想從心理分析的角度解讀您在發什麼牢騷。我猜您在暗指咱們東方受到稱讚時，絕對會回個讚美，是吧？

差不多。別忘了，您稱這為「應盡的義務」。我收你的禮，你就指望我回禮。可是，我稱讚您的時候，從不指望您也要稱讚我。

for them. Leaders who offer specific suggestions for success, not just broad-brush regurgitations of ancient proverbs.

Why is it that whenever the term *ancient* comes up, you give me the Eagle "evil eye"?

Now don't start huffing and puffing. I respect your age, and the wisdom that comes with it, and have learned that instead of backward ways, you and your Dragons are moving ahead faster than we ever dreamed possible.

You sound patronizing. What do you want?

*(shaking its head)* There you go with that ingrained cultural knee jerk reaction. (You do have knees, don't you?)

Trying to decipher your psycho-babble, I assume you are inferring that we in the East, when paid a compliment, must give you one in return?

More or less. Remember, you called it the "obligation zone." You give me a gift; I am expected to return the favor. But when I pay you a compliment, I don't expect you to give me one in return.

可是，您不能否認從新的角度看「互惠」是好的。古羅馬人不管做什麼，背後似乎都藏著自私的動機。他們稱之為「*利益交換*」。以物易物。可是，我們可以樹立新典範，不但以禮相待，也透過互惠，單純地表達對彼此的尊重。

完全同意。我熱切希望雙方都能得到一些正面的建議，讓大家的未來都更光明。

但一開始，我們得依龍族的傳統，舉杯慶賀這次聚會。接著我們大吃一頓，然後再討論並做總結。

飛了這麼久，我不但餓，還很渴。今晚很冷，如果能喝些比茶來勁的東西就更好了。您這兒有白蘭地或香檳嗎？

*（舉起一瓶精美的酒和兩個小酒杯。低沈的笑聲，想必幾百公尺外都聽得見）*沒白蘭地也沒香檳，兄弟。我有的，是數百年來傳統必喝的一種特殊醇酒。

這是什麼？看起來沒什麼顏色，裝在有腳的烈酒杯裡。

But, admit it. It's a good idea to look at "reciprocity" in a new, positive light. The Romans seemed to do everything with an ulterior motive of self-interest. They called it *"Quid Pro Quo."* Something for something. But you and I can set a new trend by being courteous and using reciprocity as a means of simply demonstrating respect for each other.

I agree completely. And I'm eager to have each of us come away with some positive suggestions to make the future brighter for all of us.

But first, a traditional Dragon toast to our get-togethers. Then we will feast, and afterwards we can talk and draw some conclusions.

I am hungry and very thirsty, after such a long flight. And, it would be nice to having something a bit stronger than tea on such a cold evening. What do you have, brandy or champagne?

*(raising a decorative bottle and two small glasses—and chuckling with a rumble that undoubtedly could be heard hundreds of meters away)* Neither brandy nor champagne, my friend. A special elixir which has been a traditional drink of ours for centuries.

What is it? It looks colorless, and the serving glasses look like small, stemmed, shot glasses.

這叫「*茅台*」，咱們最有名的「*白酒*」，由發酵的高粱所釀造，源自十七世紀清朝時期。

比我的國家還早一百年！

您可能還記得這酒直到現代才第一次露臉。尼克森總統七二年訪問龍族時，毛主席在國宴上用的就是茅台。那也是門戶開放新政策的試金石。

是酒啊，但這酒杯為什麼才大概半個盎斯而已？

*（把酒杯倒滿）*我想敬的，是我們的首次交流達到最高潮，而且將來會持續不斷。我們會說「乾杯」，把酒一口喝光，然後把酒杯倒過來，證明真的乾了。

*乾杯！*謝謝您的熱情款待。我的媽！這一路燒下去，我連爪子都發燙了。這東西到底多烈？

It is called *"Maotai,"* our most famous *"baijiu"* or liquor, distilled from fermented sorghum and originating during our Qing Dynasty in the 17th Century.

That was a hundred years before our nation was born!

In more modern times, you may remember seeing it for the first time when Chairman Mao Zedong used the wine to entertain Richard Nixon during the state banquet for his presidential visit to Dragonland in 1972. That was the first crack toward a new Open Door policy.

So it's wine. Then why are the glasses only about 1½ ounces?

*(filling their glasses)* I propose a toast to the culmination of our initial conversations and to the prospect of many more to come. We say *"ganbei,"* which means "bottoms up" and we both swallow all the contents in one gulp and hold our glasses upside down to show the other that we did.

*Ganbei!* And thanks for the hospitality. Oh my gosh! That burned all the way down to my talons. How potent is that stuff?

*（微笑）*酒精含量百分之五十三，大概相當於你們的一百六十個標準酒精度。因為我注意到您把酒杯倒過來的時候，滴了幾滴酒，所以您得依傳統馬上再喝一杯，而且要好好一口乾得一滴不剩，免得「丟臉」。

好小子，看我的啦。*（再乾一杯）*哇，我看我待會兒需要衛星導航系統，否則今晚飛不回去。您的洞光靠這酒，就可以熱烘烘地過冬啦！還有別忘了，您比我大多了，起碼多個二公噸，能乾的茅台也應該遠比我多。

這正好可以考驗您的體力和耐力。咱們敬個九巡，所以只剩八巡，這樣每條龍和他們的九個部位都敬到了。

我已經渾身發熱，鼻竇炎也完全消了！

龍準備的豐盛菜餚，多得還可以再請五到十位賓客。龍告訴鵰菜一定要多，這樣才夠大家吃飽。鵰很驚訝菜居然有卄多道，於是有禮貌地每樣都嚐，而不是某道菜吃特別多。

第一道菜有八樣冷盤，然後是「燕窩」，龍親自為鵰服務，還表示他覺得這湯名字取得好。接下來的菜，是道盤飾精美的肉，後面是龍蝦、豬、干貝和雞，以及好幾樣健康的蔬菜。酒席進行到一半時，北平烤鴨上桌，配上切花的大蔥、甜麵醬和薄餅皮。最後一道

*(smiling)* It is 53% alcohol by volume, which is about 160 Proof where you come from. And, because I notice some drops falling from your inverted glass, it is customary for you to immediately drink another glass down and "save face" by doing a proper *"gan-bei"* and empty your glass dry in one swallow.

Here's looking at you, kid. *(downs another glass)* Wow, I'm going to need a GPS tracking system if I try to fly home later tonight. That stuff could heat your cave all winter long! And, don't forget, you're much bigger than I am by a couple of tons, so you can hold your *Maotai* a lot better than I can.

It should be a good test of your fitness and endurance. We'll make nine toasts in all, with only eight more to go, one for each of our Dragons and its nine parts.

I'm feeling warm already, and definitely have cleared the sinuses in my beak!

The Dragon had prepared a sumptuous meal enough for five or ten more guests, telling the Eagle that this was proper since there should always be more than enough to go around. The Eagle was amazed that there were more than twenty courses, so it politely sampled each one, rather than eat too much of one dish.

The first course consisted of eight cold dishes, followed by bird's-nest soup, which the Dragon served personally to the Eagle, remarking that he thought the name was appropriate. Then came a decorative meat dish followed by lobster, pork, scallops and chicken, and an array of healthy vegetables. Peking duck—with scallion brushes, *"Tian Mian"* sauce and thin pancakes—was served in the middle of the banquet. The final course was

是全魚，鵬直說這是他最喜歡的菜，而且石桌上的魚頭朝向鵬，表示酒席是為他而設的。

酒席間，龍與鵬為他們的健康、運勢與未來的共榮願景舉杯敬酒。入座之前，龍就表示吃飯時不該談重要的生意。龍族認為相互認識與讚美，才算是有禮貌。特定的生意話題，吃飯時通常是不碰的。於是他們邊談笑邊相互奉承，鵬對主人的熱情款待與滿桌佳餚，更是讚不絕口。

龍教鵬要怎麼拿筷子才正確，吃飯吃麵時要怎麼以碗就口，才容易用筷子把食物送入嘴中。鵬則回頭教龍怎麼用叉子和大湯匙把麵捲起來吃，因為根據西方的習俗，吃麵時碗或盤都必須留在桌上。

鵬一口都吃不下了。他想把盤裡的菜吃乾淨，以免得罪主人，但龍向鵬說明光溜溜的盤子代表菜不夠吃，反而有些失禮。儘管鵬覺得有一、二道菜看起來不太可口，但還是有禮貌地每道都嚐。龍將其視為一種尊重。

茶酒足菜飯飽，龍與鵬移駕到隔壁的圖書館，位於巨大岩縫內的另一個洞穴，燭光和火光把裡面照得明亮。他們在那兒坐了好幾個小時，討論這麼多個月來的所有對話內容。他們都承認彼此越瞭解，該學的就越多。或許最重要的，是他們認為互挑毛病，根本是浪費時間。

於是，雙方決定寫下一些基本觀念流傳給後代子孫。這些觀念原則不偏不倚，一體適用。龍擔任主筆，因為他在羊皮紙上書寫的功力爐火純青，又具備書法天分。雙方同意好看的字應該比較有吸引力，對讀者的影響較大。

以下就是他們與各位分享的：

a whole fish, which the Eagle mentioned was its favorite, and was placed on the stone table with its head pointed toward the Eagle, as guest of honor.

Throughout the meal, Dragon and Eagle toasted their health, their good fortune, and their hope for a prosperous future together. Dragon had mentioned as they had sat down that no important business should be discussed during dinner. In Dragonland, getting to know one another and paying value to each other is proper etiquette. Specific business is not a usual topic of dinner conversation. So they laughed and flattered each other, and the Eagle paid elaborate compliments to its host about the hospitality and the delicious food.

The Dragon showed the Eagle the proper use of chopsticks, and how to eat rice and noodles with chopsticks by holding the bowl up to its chin to make it easier to scoop them up. The Eagle reciprocated by demonstrating to the Dragon how to swirl noodles with a fork and large spoon, so that they could be eaten with the bowl or plate still on the table as is the custom in the West.

The Eagle could not eat another bite but was about to clean its plate so as not to offend its host, when the Dragon assured its guest that leaving a clean plate is perceived to mean that you were not given enough food, and might be considered a slight of etiquette. The Eagle had been polite enough to try a taste of each dish, even though it found that one or two were unappealing. This the Dragon appreciated as a sign of respect.

After eating too much, and drinking too much wine and tea, the two retired to the Dragon's library in an adjoining chamber in the immense cavern, illuminated by torches and candles. There they sat for several hours discussing all their conversations during the many months previous. They admitted that the more they knew about each other, the more there was to know. Perhaps, most importantly, they agreed that preaching to each other about the other's shortcomings would be a total wasted effort.

Instead they decided to write down some basic concepts that they could pass on to their followers, that were not unique to one, but were common to both. The Dragon did the writing, having refined the art of pen on parchment with a flair for calligraphy that both agreed might get more attention from and have more impact on their readers.

This is what they wrote to share with you:

我們相信，地球的資源豐沛，對有幸分享者而言，未來必將更加美好，但可促進社會繁榮的先祖智慧，我們必須謹記；導致他們最後衰亡的偏見與短見，我們必須摒棄。恐懼一向源自無知與對未知的疑慮。相互觀察及當面直接對話，可促進知識與互信。

我們願拋棄成見，先以開放的心胸聆聽，然後才提出意見。開口時，我們願多發問少建言。要獲得喜愛，須先學習如何受到喜愛。要獲得尊重，須先以行動證明價值。我們絕不自以為是，但願不斷精進能力。彼此的歧見，不須以無意義的行為凸顯。

我們願以堅定的品德，經營事業與人生。真正的品格，在於時時做出正確的選擇，儘管它可能造成不悅，也無法弭平傷痛，我們仍願堅持。誠實不是一件對自己有利時，才穿上的外衣。誠實就如品德一般，在黑暗中仍發揮光芒。

我們願特別關懷年長與年幼者。父母與祖父母生我養我，但有朝一日他們終將如孩子般須我們照顧。過去我們依賴他們，但在我們正開始享受獨立人生的同時，他們也可能必須依賴我們。孝順不是義務，而是核心價值。

*We believe the future—for all who share the abundance of this earth—can and will be better if we heed the wisdom of our ancestors that made their societies thrive, and abandon their prejudices and lack of foresight that ultimately led to their decay and demise. Fear is always based on ignorance and apprehension of the unknown. Studying each other, and face to face dialogue, facilitates knowledge and trust.*

*We will listen openly, without prejudgment, before we advance an opinion. When we speak we will ask more questions, and offer less advice. If we want to be loved, we must learn to be more lovable. If we want respect from others, we must earn it by being worthy of respect in our actions. We must avoid thinking like experts, but always continue to gain more expertise. We can disagree without behaving disagreeably.*

*We will conduct our business and personal lives with non-situational integrity. We define true integrity as doing what's right all the time, even though it may neither please us nor alleviate our own pain and suffering. Honesty is not a garment to be worn when appropriate or when it serves us. Like character, it shows, even in the dark.*

*We will give special attention to our elderly and to our children. The parents and grandparents who gave us the gift of life, and nurtured us when we were infants, at some point in the future, become like children to us. As we were dependent upon them, so might they become dependent upon us, just when we are beginning to enjoy our independent, adult lives. It should be more than obligation. It should be a core value.*

孩子是最珍貴的自然資源，從我們身上得到的應是根與翼，而非「奪與利」。父母的天職，在於給予孩子自信、公平與自律等「根」，讓他們能夠得到動力、目標、方向與毅力等「翼」。這些特質能讓他們勇於離巢，成為負責任的青年。我們應多與他們相處，且不該用金錢溺愛他們，畢竟金錢永遠買不到孩子的愛，也無法掩飾因無法親自付出親情而產生的罪惡感。我們留在孩子心中的價值觀，遠重於我們留給他們的房產。

最重要的，是我們必須在孩子可塑性最強的童年，做他們的好榜樣。我們都是通過觀察、模仿與重複而學習。近朱者赤，近墨者黑。在這個充斥著即時影像、訊息和膚淺偶像的時代，孩子會模仿他們最常看見的人、事與物。我們必須做個值得下一代效法的典範。

我們願盡力在科技與生態間取得平衡，並為兩者注入更多人性。科技將決定未來的市場。人才將決定誰主宰市場。人力資源及其環境間的關係脆弱，而該關係能否維繫，將決定我們的未來。我們瞭解「生活水準」不等於「生活品

*Our children—our most precious natural resource—must receive from us roots and wings, instead of "loot and things." Our role as parents is to give our children the roots of self-confidence, fairness, and self-discipline, that will allow them to gain the wings of motivation, goal-orientation and resiliency. These attributes will foster courage in them to fly from our nests as responsible, young adults. We need to spend more time with our children, and spend less money indulging them, in a veiled attempt to purchase their affection, out of guilt for not being there in person to demonstrate authentic love. What we leave in our children as values, is much more important than what we leave to them as valuables in our estates.*

*Most of all, we must be positive role models and coaches for our children during their most formative, early years. We all learn by observation, imitation and repetition. We will become that to which we are most exposed. In a world of instant access to images, information and skin-deep, celebrity heroes, our children will live what they have most often watched. We must present role models for the next generation worthy of emulating.*

*We will do our best to balance technology and ecology, and human interaction with both. Technology will rule the marketplace of the future. Human capital will determine who dominates that global marketplace. Attention to the fragile relationship between human capital and its environment will ultimately decide what kind of future we will enjoy. We understand that "standard of living" and "quality of life" are not synonymous. We all want a*

質」。我們都希望自己與窮困者未來都能提升生活水準。生活水準取決於我們累積的可用支出。生活品質取決於我們如何運用時間，以及我們處於何種環境。為了創造未來，我們瞭解健康重於財富，且尊嚴並非取決於購買能力。

我們願成為思考縝密的終生學習者，結合正規教育與孩子般熱切的好奇心，才不會僵硬地墨守成規。我們必須運用「高科技」的研究、溝通與組織能力，以培養求知求真的精神與創新的行事方法。我們也必須盡力提供「人性化」的服務與無私的關懷，才不會變得無趣而僵化。科技是不帶情感的。

我們願讚頌雙方的共同目標，並接納雙方的差異，同時謹記自己的方法，未必是最好的方法。享有任何權利之前，我們必須先採取有價值的行動。我們珍惜的任何權利，都附帶著相對須履行的義務。為享有自由，個人與全體均須負起責任，承受自我選擇後應得的善果或惡果。這一切，我們永遠會歡喜樂觀的加以實踐。

雙方在此署名見證之。

龍：　　　　　　　　　　鵰：

higher standard of living for our impoverished masses and for ourselves. Standard of living is the amount of money we accumulate to spend. Quality of life is how we spend our time, and in what environment. In order to have a future, we must realize that health means more than wealth, and that human dignity is not based on purchasing power.

We will become life-long learners and critical thinkers, combining formal education with the passionate curiosity of children, who have not been told they must always color inside the lines. We must develop the capacity to seek knowledge and truth, and new ways to do things, by becoming more "high tech" in our research and in our communication and organizational processes. We must also embrace the idea of becoming "high-touch" service providers and gracious caregivers so that we don't become jaded and robotic in nature. There is nothing intimate about technology.

We must celebrate our mutual desires, and appreciate our differences, mindful that our way is not necessarily the best way. For every privilege we desire, we must provide a worthy action. For every right that we cherish, there is a duty we must perform. Freedom will always carry the price of individual and collective responsibility and the just rewards or consequences of our own choices.

And we do all this in the spirit of joy and eternal optimism.

Signed,

The Dragon The Eagle

龍放下筆和紙捲，抬頭尋求鵬的認可。

*（將正本交給鵬）*鵬兄，不妨提出您的看法？

絕對是個開始而已。

但現在還只能光說，對吧？

沒錯。我們都知道光說無益，且光說的一定比願意練的多。民眾要的，是貫徹到底的行動

只有時間，才能告訴我們這些對話是寓言，還是事實。

*（轉身跳向洞穴的入口）*您的下一步怎麼走？

第一次見面時我就說過，我不住這兒。我只是過來清清蜘蛛網，打個坐而已。大多數的時間，我都在各省的大城市與小農村裡。我們成長得如此迅速，要跟上轉型期間的這一切變化，挑戰性實在非常

The Dragon put down its pen and scroll and looked up at the Eagle for confirmation.

*(handing Eagle an original copy)* A *yuan* for your thoughts, Eagle?

It's certainly a beginning.

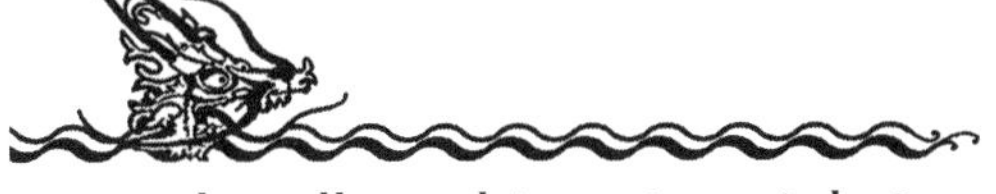

But only talk at this point, right?

Exactly. We both know that talk is cheap, and that supply exceeds demand. What our constituents want is action and follow through.

Only time will tell whether our conversations are fable or factual.

*(turning and hopping toward the entrance of the cave)* So where do you go from here?

As I said when we first met, I don't live here. I only come here to clear the cobwebs and meditate. I spend my time in big cities and small, rural villages in each of our provinces. We are growing so rapidly that it is very challenging to keep up with all the changes

高。下次我倆一定要再來次空中導覽，飛越農村與城市，讓您親眼看看我國真正的轉變。

老朋友，這太好了。同樣的，我也想邀請您和所有龍族的伙伴來訪。我們正在試著清理環境，為開發中國家做個更好的榜樣。您一定能從我們的錯誤和進步中學到許多。

我承諾會大聲呼籲我國國民，不論老幼，都考慮學習你們的語言，研究你們的歷史與文化。甚至我自己都想上普通話的會話課，這樣就比較聽得懂你們的諺語和敬酒詞。感謝您在我到訪時都說英文。我們常以為大家說英文是理所當然的，並自傲地拒絕去瞭解朋友與其它國家的行事方法。

鵰兄，這才叫智慧。我們的孩子都必須把英文做為第二語言，所以懂多種語言者會越來越多。我們其實住在一個無國界的世界，其中唯一不變的，就是變化永不停息。

您的知無不言與熱情款待，讓我感到我們之間的距離並不重要。可是，天將破曉，我得飛回我在西方山上的家了。您都讓我改喝茶了，而且改的還不止於此。

說不定我們下次可以約在星巴克™，由您來介紹些特別的咖啡給我嚐嚐。咱們這兒的時髦的咖啡廳，都快跟貴國一樣多了。

that are taking place in our transformation. Next time we should take another aerial tour of the countryside and cities so you can see the real transformation for yourself.

I would like that, my friend, and the same invitation is open to you and all other Dragons. We are trying to clean up our environment and set a better example for developing economies. You can learn much from our mistakes and our progress.

I promise to urge our citizens, young and old, to consider learning your language and studying your history and culture. I may even take a class in conversational Mandarin myself, so I can understand some of your favorite proverbs and toasts more easily. I appreciate your kindness in speaking English during my visits. We tend to take for granted that everybody speaks English, while we complacently resist making the effort to learn the ways of our friends and of other nations.

That would be wise, Eagle. All of our children are required to learn English as a second language, and many of them are becoming multilingual. In reality, we live in a borderless world in which change is the only constant.

Thanks to these conversations, and your gracious hospitality, I feel the distance between us has become irrelevant. But, it will soon be dawn and I must fly back to my nest on the mountain in the West. You've made a tea drinker out of me. And that's not all.

Perhaps we can meet at a Starbucks™ next time and you can introduce me to some special coffees. We have almost as many of your swank coffee houses here as you have in your own country.

你們很快就會比我們更富足了。早見面比晚見面好。您說得好，這不過是開場的結尾而已。

鵰優雅地揮翼升空，然後低空從龍穴前飛過。鵰行了個軍禮，向他的新朋友道別，不斷盤旋上升沒入灰暗的冬夜中。

龍目送著，直到鵰變成暗黃月色前的一個小黑點為止。然後龍轉身緩緩回到地面的大岩縫中，深切期盼那些對話的意義能夠延續，而不會淪為一堆茶渣和憐憫而已。

**Soon you'll have more of everything than we have. Let's make it sooner than later. As you said, this is but the end of the beginning.**

Flapping its wings gracefully, the Eagle took flight, and made one low pass in front of the Dragon's lair. Then with a soldier's salute, bid farewell to its new friend, and circled higher and higher in the grey winter sky.

The Dragon watched until Eagle became a tiny silhouette against a pale, yellow moon. It then turned and slowly returned to the great crevice in the earth, hoping against hope these exchanges would have lasting significance, and not be regarded simply as tea and sympathies.

# 後記
# Epilogue

中國已站穩腳步，並注定成為最偉大的世界經濟強權之一，甚至稱之為最偉大者亦不為過。中國的經濟力量，在可預見的未來，會將近是美國的二倍，相當於北美、歐洲與日本的總和。這是事實，而非幻想。眼前的挑戰還很多，且這條路絕不平順。中國在經濟、文化及地緣政治方面的影響力，將以驚人的速度達到顛峰，若對此有所懷疑者，僅要到東南亞四處考察，就一定有機會親眼目睹這個人口最多的國家，是如何經歷這段蛻變的過程。此一成就，是文明史上最能彰顯人類創意與毅力的卓越典範之一。欲維繫這股活力，中國必須運用智慧解析其成就，以解決現代新興城市窮富極貴，而偏遠地區卻民窮財匱的懸殊問題。

☆☯☆☯☆☯☆☯☆☯☆☯☆☯☆☯☆☯☆☯☆☯☆☯☆☯☆☯☆☯☆☯☆

☯☆☯☆☯☆☯☆☯☆☯☆☯☆☯☆☯☆☯☆☯☆☯☆☯☆☯☆☯☆☯☆☯☆

The United States of America has enjoyed unprecedented growth and development in but a few hundred years as a nation. It has more patents, inventions, innovations, personal freedoms and wealth than many industrialized countries combined. The United States is a tapestry of pioneers and entrepreneurs, most of them immigrants, leaving environments of poverty and oppression, in search of opportunity for themselves and their families. Undeniably, it is the greatest success story ever experienced by a modern society. To remain competitive in this *new world* and to continue its winning record of achievements, it must motivate its youth to study the sciences that will spearhead future technology, and refocus on the virtues, work ethic, and principles upon which its foundation was built.

China is poised and destined to become one of the greatest—if not *the* greatest—economic world powers. In the foreseeable future the economy of China will be nearly twice as large as that of the U.S. and equal to the combined economies of all North America, Europe and Japan. This is reality, not fantasy. There are many challenges ahead and the journey promises to be anything but smooth. Those who doubt the amazing ascendancy of China to the zenith of economic, cultural and geopolitical influence would be well served to spend time traveling throughout Southeast Asia to witness, first hand, the metamorphosis of our most populous nation. It is one of the most awesome examples of human ingenuity and perseverance in recorded history. To sustain this momentum, it will need to digest its success with wisdom, balancing the appetites for wealth in its burgeoning, modern cities, with the very real hunger of its rural masses.

美利堅合眾國立國雖僅數百年，但卻享有前所未見的成長與發展。美國擁有的專利、發明、創意、個人自由與財富，超過許多工業國家的總和。美國彷彿一幅交織著拓荒者與企業家的壁飾，其中大多是移民，為逃離貧窮與壓迫，離鄉背井為自己和家人找尋機會。現代美國社會歷經的成就，無疑是最偉大的成功故事。為在這個新世界保持競爭力，並延續其無以比擬的成就，美國必須鼓勵年輕人研究將在未來引領風潮的科技，並重拾美德、職業道德等當初立國的根基。

## 衛禮的其它著作

勝利者的優勢
致勝心理學
卓越的種子
追求卓越
雙贏
偉大的時刻
時機決定一切
新世紀致勝之道
成功人生的九大強力秘訣
激勵心理學
新世紀達標之道
心智王國
卓越的種子寶庫
心靈之旅

**衛禮的合著**

樂在工作
光速健身之道
創意致勝之道
快樂退休之道
永續企業
女性之致勝心理學

**欲瞭解**衛禮的專題演講、訓練課程及其它視聽與線上服務，請按下列方式索取資料：

地址： **The Waitley Institute**
P.O. Box 197
Rancho Santa Fe, California 92067
電話： 1-800-WAITLEY
電郵： info@waitley.com

或前往：**www.waitley.com**

## Other Books by Denis Waitley

The Winner's Edge
The Psychology of Winning
The Seeds of Greatness
Being the Best
The Double Win
Moments of Greatness
Timing is Everything
The New Dynamics of Winning
Nine Empowering Secrets of Successful Living
The Psychology of Motivation
The New Dynamics of Goal Setting
Empires of the Mind
The Seeds of Greatness Treasury
Safari to the Soul

**Denis Waitley's Co-authored Books:**

The Joy of Working
Quantum Fitness
Winning the Innovation Game
How to be Happily Retired
The Future-Proof Corporation
The Psychology of Winning for Women

**For information** on Denis Waitley's keynote lectures, seminars and other audio-visual and online services, please contact:


## The Waitley Institute

P.O. Box 197
Rancho Santa Fe, California 92067
Phone: 1-800-WAITLEY
E-mail: info@waitley.com

Or visit:
**www.waitley.com**